From: Dr. Joe Grana

"Bob Alexander demonstrates a pastor's heart in his, *"Religion: A Brief History."* He stays true to the title by clearly summarizing the world's religions along with their leaders and unique contributions to the religious landscape. He gives an insightful synopsis of history, biography, and statistics. Bob's approach is factual and fair. HE IS INFORMATIVE AND RESPECTIVE. His book is a helpful read for those wanting an overview of such a deep and important topic."

Dr. Joseph C. Grana II, Dean
Pacific Christian College of Ministry & Biblical Studies
Hope International University, Fullerton, California

From: Paul Cedar

"I am impressed with your book. I believe it has great potential to be used by pastors and other church leaders for an initial 'read through,' but also as a very helpful reference book. IT SHOULD BE A VERY HELPFUL RESOURCE FOR ALL WHO READ IT."

Paul Cedar; D.Min, D.D., Phd
Former positions:
Chairman and Chief Executive Officer, Mission America Coalition
President, Evangelical Free Church of America
Senior Pastor, Lake Ave Church, Pasadena, California

From: Tom Lawell

"Having spent thirty years in our United States Air Force I didn't have much time to study the Bible, attend Bible study classes or at times even attend church. Now that I am retired I have spent many hours reading the Bible, attending three Bible studies a week, church on Sunday's and watching many DVDs concerning world religions. Recently I had an opportunity to review Pastor Robert Alexander's new book and found it to be one of the most complete and factual books on world religions I have ever been exposed to. Robert's explanations of the early Christian church's development and the Romans Catholic influences was very enlightening. His Chapter 4 covering the Islam religion should be a must read for everyone. It is the fastest growing religion in the world and will have a great impact on world religions in the 21st century and beyond. In chapter 10 Robert discusses the challenges of all religions in the future times. In summary, I found Pastor Robert Alexander's book to be one of the most complete and factual books on world religions I have ever been exposed to. I highly recommend his book to anyone interested in this most important subject."

Tom Lawell
Colonel, USAF, (retired)

Religion; a Brief History

Controversies and Challenges

Robert H. Alexander

Publisher: tte publishing—Desert Hot Springs, CA
ISBN: 978-0-692-07957-7
Card Catalogue Number: 2018940481
Title: Religion, a Brief History | Controversies and Challenges
Robert H. Alexander
Digital distribution | (Pending), 2017.
Paperback Edition | 2017

About the Author

ROBERT H. ALEXANDER, A.B., M.A., D.D. author

A native Oklahoman, Dr. Alexander has served churches in pastoral ministries for over five decades. Other professional services include: a Christian College presidency; CEO of a denominational development fund; ownership of a church capital stewardship services company. As a stewardship Consultant, and in addition to related organizational activities, he has also preached in over forty of these congregations, representing a broad scope of denominational fellowships.

Teaching: His seminars include studies in church history, ancient religions and modern religious controversies which give background to this book, "Religion, A Brief History, Controversies and Challenges."
Recognition and Honors: Past President, Southern Christian Convention; Founder of the Oklahoma Christian Convention; Closing night speaker, North American Christian Convention; Board of Trustees: Los Robles Regional Medical Center, Thousand Oaks, California; Past Chairman, Board of Trustees, Pacific Christian College, (now Hope International University); Double Paul Harris Fellow, Rotary International; Bob Alexander Day, Muskogee, Oklahoma; Alumnus of the Year, Atlanta Christian College, (now Point University).

He and his wife Peggy live in Desert Hot Springs, California

Dedication

Dedicated to my parents (now deceased) who first introduced me to the church and whose devotion to it has been a constant inspiration. Also, to my wife Peggy, whose faith, encouragement and patience has kept me centered and focused.

Religion; a Brief History

Controversies and Challenges

Table of Contents

Robert H. Alexander A.B., M.A., D.D. author
"Bob Alexander"

RELIGION: a Brief History

Modern Controversies and Challenges

Robert H. Alexander

Preface

This book is written by a preacher/teacher both as a source of information for the interested layman and a handy reference for teachers and students. There is no attempt to interpret the belief systems of the greater religions of the world, nor is there any attempt to quantify the effectiveness of their mission. My purpose is to promote a better understanding among peoples of diverse beliefs.

I have tried to give a brief overview of the origin, major leaders, doctrines and history of the leading beliefs of the world. In addition, I have dedicated a large portion of the book to:

1. Controversies that are presently allowing deep divisions in the church at large.
2. Challenges facing the modern American church.

I thank those who have reviewed parts or all of the content. Statistics have been checked carefully. Any errors in either the representations of beliefs or their statistics are solely mine.

R.H.A.

Desert Hot Springs, California

RELIGION: A BRIEF HISTORY
PROLOGUE

It is said that those who write about religion tend to have an axe to grind. This study is intended to be objective, treating religious historical data and institutional expressions from a position of neutrality, although philosophically sound, this neutrality may be in practice, challenging.

Early observations:

'Religions' are a dime a dozen with always room for one more in the spiritual marketplace. The game most always changes when a new creed starts threatening the profits and privilege of the established set ups.

Violence purportedly carried out in the name of God is nearly always in reality caused by other factors-political, social, racial, and or especially economic. A recent public television series, "Money," was in fact a reality show with this thesis, "Money is the dynamic of humankind, within evely historical and present-day experience." Money, they defined, is the barter (trade) system of physical life, without which nothing happens. They suggested that even a discussion of religion in any sense of its universality, would not be relevant without 'trade' that allowed missionaries to board ships taking their religion to far off lands. While this intriguing proposition demands thoughtful analysis, its broadness may not pass inspection.

If I may offer a parallel synopsis: If money is the commodity of physical humanity, Religion is the commodity of spiritual humanity. Religion: "The anvil that has worn out many hammers-an instinct for survival."

Chapter 1

The History of Religion

Religion is found in the field of the supernormal and may be defined as a link between the infinite or as a grasping by man toward something beyond himself which gives him a reason for being. In this study we assume that religion has been common to all men from earliest times. The crises which early man had to face were the origin or the fountainhead of our modem sacraments.

Religion had its birth in the fears of early man. Among the earliest primitives there were two kinds of spirits only; hostile spirits and neutral spirits. Only later came a belief in good or helpful forces, and the idea of 'God'. To appease or hide from the evil or angry spirits, among other things, the use of disguises, rituals and fetishes or through the kindly offices of a shaman or "medicine man" came into practice.

The next step was the setting up an idol or totem. Then a house for the idol and the first 'church' appeared on the stage. The medicine man became the idol tender or priest. To maintain his power, the priest built up a complicated ritual which only he and a chosen few could properly perform. To them there were many ways to go or do wrong but only one way of going right, and they alone possessed the skills, knowledge or intelligence to fully perform these rituals. Later this developed into a system of beliefs and secrets of which 1st century Gnosticism is an example.

The importance of early religion should not be under-estimated. It had the same efficacy as have some higher forms. It required faith, and faith restored self-confidence, which in tum made the seemingly hopeless possible of attainment.

Following came gifts; gifts to the totem or idol. Gifts were the origin of sacrifice. Things most precious to man were thought to be almost precious to the god. Even life itself became a common expression of "the best gift." In addition to the priest's power came the new religio-science of tabu (later spelled taboo)-the thing forbidden. He taught that there were many evil spirits extant that should be avoided; thus the term "forbidden"; examples: aversion to certain animal flesh, marriage with a close relative, incest, murder, cursing one's father, kindling a fire on a holy day, touching a corpse and eating at certain periods. Many have survived to modem times (negative type tabu).

Tabu was often a primitive means of gaining a socially desirable end. Sooner or later people find that commission of a breach of tabu does not bring catastrophe in its wake, and this leads to carelessness. Examples of 'positive type tabu' can be found among certain tribes where initiatory ceremonies of young men at puberty amounts to their education-a passing on of the knowledge and customs of the tribe from the old men to the young. Here the ceremonies when more carefully observed derived good.

Ideas of religion change as man's type of civilization changes. Thus, we find corresponding differences in the beliefs and ritual as man progresses from hunting to pastorals to agricultural stages in social advance. Old magic rites remain but are linked more definitely with specific things in the way of life. We find seedtime and harvest connected to festivals.

Seedtime: festivals essentially were lewd and sensual. Harvest; festivals among farmers were primarily ones of thanksgivings; rites connected with sacrifice such as "First fruits,". abundant crops. animal sacrifices for herds and flocks. and human sacrifices for good health and

2

preservation of the tribe. Later human sacrifices, associated with seedtime were associated with death and resurrection.

To the nomads, the stars and sun were more important and became the special objects of veneration. They substituted effigies or dummies for animal sacrifices probably because of their poverty. There were no temples and no priests as they were wanderers. The main events in life called for festivals; birth, circumcision, a form of infant baptism, puberty, marriage and burial.

A changed attitude towards gods is found, too, as man becomes more civilized. There is a definite tendency to persuade the gods to do man's will instead of trying to force them. The priest increased in importance as a result.

Celts: One of the best example of early sun and fire worshipers. Mistletoe was an object of their veneration because it grew between earth and sky with no visible roots. The oak was respected because it supported the mistletoe. The places of worship therefore became first, groves of oak, and secondly, circles of stone representative of a grove. Best known of these is STONEHENGE, ENGLAND. Some have dated Stonehenge to 1700 B.C. Recent excavation indicates a much earlier date, probably in the late Neolithic period prior to the use of metal tools. As tribes fused, so gods were fused. Thus, the chief gods became composites, often with composite names thus thought to appease the polytheism of multiple tribes. Later these gods were thought to exact penalties for undetected crimes, crimes thus becoming a 'sin,' Since no visible punishment was visited on the criminal led to the belief in a future life of punishment. Long after this belief developed, did the idea of a future life of rewards occur to man.

Special rites were usually connected with sacrifice. Rites

of priestesses were of a sexual nature, All festivals were marked with great bonfires and sex orgies in the fields. Their festivals have survived in our Halloween, All Saints Day, Maypole dances, May-day celebrations, Lugnasad in Midsummer Night and St John's Day festivals.

In any study of Religion and its history, it must include a study of the manifestations of religion, i.e. the institutions of religion. A study of these institutions and how religion affects them is an objective pursuit, whereas the study of 'stand-alone' religion is subjective by its very nature; the relationship of man and God

The nature of religion suggests an inner constitution and meaning, which thoughtful men over the ages haven striven in vain to discover. It is a fundamental tenet of most believers that seeking and striving, in themselves, lead nowhere, that the truth that sets men free is other than, and apart from, all human striving. Among the approaches to the subject of religious truth that bring some measure of understanding of it are those afforded by the study of comparative religion, and the examination· of such concepts as grace and faith, the image of God, and the solidarity of mankind.

Comparative Religion

The canons of the study of comparative religion are basically three:

First, when any given religion is studied objectively it is set forth in the light of its own affirmations, dogmatics, claims, apologetics and the ethical performance that it fosters.

Second, such a study proceeds based on understanding history, theology, and social dynamics, to describe the radical differences between the several faiths. The study should presuppose a reverent attitude, sympathy, and appreciation, and view each religion as a bridge to the truth, as evidence of man's incurable spiritual nature. One may not prejudge the merits of a given religion or to state in advance its superiority over another.

Third, equally valid would be the presupposition that all religions are equally true, or their differences do not really matter. In this connection, the findings of scholarship and criticism are indispensable. The Greeks who found the world "full of Gods" were yet by the power of reason and rational thought bound to rid themselves of much superstition and mythology.

Present-day religious institutions will dominate the latter half of this study; their belief systems, societal expressions, and major causes that has led to deep divisions within its ranks. Religion has never been more banned, blamed or extolled than in the last one hundred years. Will religion survive the next century?

An ancient Russian saying: "Life is short; the Volga is long; man's need for religion is eternal."

Grace and Faith

Grace and faith constitute the underpinning of religion. The truth of religion finds justification in the gift of grace and in faith, the means of articulation. Religion relies upon God for the illumination of the dark recesses of the heart and for the revelation of the truth of heaven to selfish souls. The inward religious crisis is reached when, overwhelmed by God's gift of grace, a man like Paul surrenders in submission and faith, saying, "Here I am Lord, lead me", and later, "Yet not I, but Christ liveth in me."

The Image of God

Thomas Aquinas maintained that the "image of God," as man's relation of obedience and love to God, was destroyed by the fall of man from the state of perfection. In his opinion, the "image of God" cannot be construed as part of man's original nature but rather as a "supernatural gift." In the end, conscious of his being created in the divine image, man refuses to worship a God created in his own image, for a creature is unwilling to worship a mere projection of his own fallible nature.

Human Solidarity

The intricate mysteries of man, matter, and God, are not rendered less mysterious by pooling eastern and western insights, or fractional faiths, or denominational structures. The contribution of religion to the unity of all human beings is made, then, not in the intellectual but in the spiritual realm. In the memorable adoration of St. Augustine, "Thou has created us, O God, for thyself and restless are our souls until they find their rest in thee," God is acknowledged not only as the ally but also as the spiritual leader of all mankind.

Early Religions of the Far East;
Taoism, Shintoism, and Zoroastrianism

Early records in China revealed an advanced animism (a belief that all things, even the universe have souls or spirits) which was almost monotheistic. The symbol for the supreme being signifies "Great One" and is often translated "Heaven." Worship was usually associated with the more prominent objects of nature such as the sun, the moon, or a river.

There two sacrificial rituals. One belonged to the religion of the state and was directed toward the Supreme Being. Since there was no priest class in ancient China, the only performer was the Emperor, and the sacrifice was usually annual.

The other sacrifice was addressed to the spirits of the dead, and any father could perform these rites. The sacrifice was for prayer and thanksgiving. Devotion to the dead became the keynote of early Chinese worship. Ancestor worship later waned as it was regarded as a bar to progress because it was backward looking. It never was a prayer for the dead, as that would be an insult to one's ancestors. The sacrifice was simply an act of honor. This rite did show a belief in the existence of life after death, but their religion never indicated the kind of existence, especially for the wicked. Good and ill acts of the parents were thought to be rewarded and punished in the children-a doctrine that could be compared to the Judaic teaching of reward and punishment "even to the third generation."

Taoism

One of the great Chinese religious founders was Lao-Tse, born just at the beginning of the sixth century B. C. The sixth was an important century because it produced Lao-Tse, Confucius, Gautama, Mahavira and Zoroaster. The followers of Lao-Tse became known as Taoists, and the belief as Taoism. With no gods it was a high-toned philosophy. As an old man Lao-tse summarized his teaching in a five-thousand-word treatise, which later became the Taoist's Bible, bearing the title Tao-Teh-King. It is divided into two sections, the first to explain the why of the universe, the second, the how of life. Taoism inculcated goodness, simplicity, spontaneity, and gentleness in everyday life.

While Confucius taught reciprocity, Lao-Tse taught return good for evil, and this five hundred years before Christ. Early apologists claimed the Tao books' teaching however were so philosophical and aloof, that they could not hold the common man. The disciples that followed made it a ritual only and made the Tao-Teh-King as a source of magic. By the second century, Tao-Teh himself had been deified and was worshiped with sacrifice. Modem Taoism is a system of unreasoning credulity based on superstition, a foolish idolatry served by an ignorant and venal priesthood.

Shintoism

Shinto, the national religion of Japan is not really a religion at all, but it is the oldest and one of the simplest of creeds. It rose out of hero worship, the essential principle being ancestor worship. Shinto means, "Way of the Spirits."

It is a religio-political system which has neither sacred books nor a moral code; which extends only to the subjects of Mikado and which recognizes no distinction between its mythology and the history of the nation. It treats no future state and knows neither a paradise nor a hell; Shinto embraces the Imperial Dynasty of Japan as a part of the godhead, thus giving then Emperor divine right to rule his subjects.

The central shrine of Shinto is at Ise, in central Japan. Pilgrimages are made here as an excuse for a great merrymaking, ending in all the vicious attractions of the nearby city of Yamada with its saloon and brothels. Deities are numberless.

The best that can be said about Shinto is that there were never bloody sacrifices or cruel or immoral 1ituals. It has no appeal to any instinct of good or evil and is hollow and empty, promising no definite destiny. What its future will be since decades ago Emperor Hirohito renounced his claim to divinity is still to be determined.

Zoroastrianism

Out of Persia was to come one of the highest and most philosophic conceptions of deity before the time of Christ. The Persians started with the same animistic primitive tendencies as other people of their time, but about 660 B.C. a man-child was born in Media, a neighboring state, who was to bring forth a highly esteemed and enlightened religion. This was Zarathustra or Zoroaster. He was, according to legend a wonder child born of an immaculate conception, who attained salvation suddenly and peached a religion well suited to the needs of the people on the Iranian plateaus with their tough struggle for survival.

He taught that life was a struggle between the forces of Good and Evil, the world being the battleground on which there could be no neutrals. Each man must choose which side on which he would stand, and in making the choice he must bear in mind the judgment hereafter. No mercy could be shown the enemy. Good works were admired and encouraged. Thus, did Zoroaster give for the first time in history an answer to the question, "What is life?" He said, "To fight for the right." They believed in paradise and a hell. Both ends were continuance of thought, word and deeds, either good or bad, one to holiness, the other unto physical torment.

In the days of the end-time all the dead would be restored by a savior born of the seed of Zoroaster and a virgin who was to conceive in a lake impregnated with his semen. The good and the evil would join in a great battle known as "The affair," from which, after a period of doubt and darkness, Ahura Mazda would emerge victorious. Then all the hills and mountains would melt and pour over the earth in a great flood. Every wicked thing would perish as though scalded, but the righteous would wade through with laughter, as through in a bath of warm milk. The earth would then be a paradise with no mountains or deserts, no savages or wild breasts, where the just would live on forever with joy and gladness in their hearts.

Later spumed by his people, the Medes, Zoroaster took his beliefs to Persia. He was not accepted here either, but by 500 B.C. Zoroastrianism had become the leading faith of the Persians.

The most numerous sect of Zoroastrianism existent today is the Parsees in Indian numbering about 90,000. They are the descendants of those Persians who, in the seventh and eighth centuries were permitted to settle in India.

Their religion is a universal monotheism. It imposes love of God, love of truth, and charity in all its connotations. Its influence on both Judaism and Christianity is easily noted. The Affair colors accounts of the last days in both the Old and New Testaments. Mithraism, (god of Light) a direct outgrowth of Zoroastrianism was adapted in large part to Christian teachings and rituals. This ancient religion remained culturally present in Roman history up through the fifth century. Two rituals; initiatory baptism and the Eucharist were practiced. Debate continues among historians as to which sacramental system influenced the other; Christian over Mithraism or Mithraism over Christian.

Ancient Religious faith; Buddhism

Another Hindu, who was to become the founder of an entirely new branch of religion was Siddhartha Gautama. Born about 560 B.C. into riches and nobility and then living a riotous life at 28 he gave that up and married.

Shortly after his son was born, he left behind his riches and family to seek Nirvana. For six years he still found no peace. On one day sitting in meditation under a banyan tree, he caught a vision of the way of salvation. From this day forward, he became the Buddha "the Enlightened One," and a new religion was born.

Buddhism had its source, like Hinduism, in the Upanishads, but rejected much of Brahminic doctrine. Gautama discounted the authority of much of their old laws, caste, priesthood, theology and rituals. The Buddhist stresses moral living much more than ritualism. Mahavira stresses salvation for the individual, Gautama for the masses. The command of Gautama, "Go ye now out of compassion for the world and preach the doctrine which is glorious" could be compared to the New Testament commandment of Christ, "Go ye into all the world and preach the gospel." Buddhism with Islam and Christianity is the third great missionary religion.

11

In the Vinaya Pitaks are three sets of rules for perfecting their mind. One, their Ten Commandments, could be compared to the Mosaic table in the Old Testament. Each one begins with, "Thou shall not..." The ninth one might have been hard to handle, "thou shall not sleep on a broad, comfortable bed."

Buddhism did not spread rapidly until the third century, when missionaries were sent throughout India. The system depreciated from a high moral to a theological dogma with Gautama a god, and Nirvana a post mortem heaven. Much paganism and alien ritual were added. Today pure Buddhism is found only in Siam, Ceylon and Burma.

The birth of the Buddha
From the Harvard Classics

Translated from the Introduction to the Ja'taka (a biography of Buddha)

"Now while the future Buddha was still dwelling in the city of the Tusita gods, the "Buddha Uproar," as it is called, took place. For there are three uproars which take place in the world, the Cyclic-Uproar, the Buddha-Uproar, and the Universal-Monarch-Uproar." To paraphrase: The gods called Lokabyuhas, inhabitants of a heaven of sensual pleasure, wander through the world, weeping, hair flying and in great disorder. They make this announcement, "Sirs, after the lapse of a hundred thousand years, the cycle is to be renewed: the world will be destroyed, burnt up ... Therefore, sirs, cultivate friendliness, compassion, joy, and indifference; wait on your mothers, wait on your fathers, honor your elders." This is called Cyclic-Uproar.

"Again, when it is known that after the lapse of a

thousand years, an omniscient Buddha is to arise in the world, the guardian angels of the world wander about, proclaiming: Sirs, after a lapse of a thousand years Buddha will arise in the world." This is called the Buddha-Uproar.

"And lastly, when they realize that after a lapse of a hundred years a Universal Monarch is to arise, the terrestrial deities wander about, proclaiming: "Sirs, after the lapse of a hundred years a Universal Monarch is to arise in the world." This is called the Universal-Monarch-Uproar.

When of these three Uproars they hear the sound of the Buddha-Uproar, the gods of all ten thousand worlds come together into one place and having ascertained what particular being is to be The Buddha, they approach him, and beseech him to become one. But it is not until after omens have appeared that they beseech him; saying, "Sir, it was not to acquire the glory of a Sakka, or of a Mara, or of a Brama, or of the Universal Monarch. that you fulfilled the Ten Perfections; but it was to gain omniscience to save the world, that you fulfilled-them. Sir, the time and fit season for your Buddhaship has arrived."

But the Great Being, before assenting to their wish, made what is called the five great observations. He observed, namely, the time, the continent, the country, the family, and the mother and her span of life.

Note" once the first four had been determined, the most interesting 'observation', is that of selecting his mother to be.

Then he observed concerning his mother; "The mother of Buddha," thought he, "is never a wanton, nor a drunkard, but is one who has fulfilled the perfection through a hundred thousand cycles, and has kept the five percepts unbroken from the day of her birth. Now this queen Maha-Maya is such a one; and she shall be my mother. But what shall the span of her life?" And he perceived it to be ten months and seven days.

Surrounded by the gods of the Tusita heaven, and being continually reminded of his accumulated merit, the gods said, "attain in your next existence your high destiny." Now it is while they kept reminding him of his merits that he died and was conceived in the womb of queen Maha-Maya. This is the matter of his conception: The queen fell asleep and dreamed the following dream; the four guardian angels came and lifted her up and took her away to the Himalaya Mountains. Then the wives of the angels came and conducted her to Anotatta Lake, and bathed her, to remove every stain. And after clothed her with divine garments and anointed her with perfumes and decked her out with divine flowers. They spread her out on a divine couch with its head to the east.

Now the future Buddha had become a superb white elephant, and was wandering about and approaching from the north, he plucked a white lotus with his silvery trunk, and trumpeting loudly, went into the golden mansion. And three times he walked around his mother's couch, with his right side towards it, and striking her on her right side, he seemed to enter her womb. Then the conception took place in the Midsummer Festival.

Now the instant the Future Buddha was conceived in the womb of his mother, all the ten thousand worlds suddenly quaked, quivered and shook. An immeasurable light spread through the ten thousand worlds; the blind recovered their sight, as if to see this his glory; the deaf received their hearing; the dumb talked, the hunchback became straight of body; the lame recovered the power to walk; prisoners were set free; the fifes went out in all the hells; all instruments gave forth their notes without being played upon; celestial music was heard to play in the sky.

And whereas a Womb that had been occupied by the Future Buddha is like the shrine of a temple, and can never be occupied or used again, therefore, it was that the mother of the Future Buddha died when he was seven days old and was reborn in the Tusita heaven.

Shinnyo-Buddhism

In an article from a local newspaper on Mother's Day, 2017, the writers, a married couple and Shinnyo Buddhist practitioners, gave an insightful look at why Buddhists honor the day well beyond the secular adoration most common on Mother's Day.

They explained that the month of May, was the birth month of Shinnyo co-founder with Master Tomoji Ito, known as a Dharma Mother and spiritual source. May was also the month for change and transformation. They desired to honor Mother's Day by being mindful that Master Tomoji was the mother to everyone.

"Tomoji became keenly aware as a young girl of hers and other people's suffering. She married Shinjo Ito and together they raised six children and had a happy life. Yet they were destined toward a spiritual path that would give greater meaning beyond material prosperity and security. They dedicated their lives to the service of others. After the Itos enshrined a sacred image of Buddha, they went through 30 days of winter austerities. Following this rigorous training, Tomoji was guided to seek beyond the exoteric into the esoteric, master the way correctly, and for the sake of people and the world, carry through to the very end. After mastering Shingon Esoteric Buddhism they established a new Buddhist order in 1936. Finding support in the Nirvana Sutra, they stressed that both lay, and clergy would equally train in the aspiration for spiritual.

The article ends with the couple giving an understandable summary of Shinnyo Buddhism: "The aim is to develop one's profoundly subtle spiritual capabilities through the practice of (1) service, (2) offerings, (3) sharing the teachings, through which one can develop and heighten the state of mind."

Confucianism

Known by the Latin form of his name, Confucius. He was born in 551 B.C., a decedent of the Shang dynasty. Married in his early twenties, Confucius remained monogamous throughout his life and became father of a son and two daughters. Politically active he became a magistrate of a state. This state came so near of becoming a model state, that his superiors became so jealous that he was dismissed from his position. For many years afterward, he wandered about the country side homeless and in want. In the spring of 478 B.C. he died at the age of 73.

He was not a founder, but a simple man and sage of simple, practical wisdom. Not a religious man, he was a student of ancient beliefs who observed and passed on his knowledge. He felt himself to have a mission inspired by love of mankind. He was a closer parallel to the Hebrew Solomon of the Old Testament than to any of the founders of religions.

Confucius stressed the importance of learning, loyalty, ethics, and truthfulness and urged caution in fasting, making war, and treatment of disease. His highest contribution was in the field of ethics. In society he perceived five relationships and outlined the proprieties to be observed in each-between husband and wife, parent and child, elders and youth, rulers and subjects, friend and friend. He formulated a Golden rule of reciprocity, "What

you do not want done to yourself, do not to others,"
At his death his sayings were collected and written down in the Analects. In 1907 he became one of the prime deities of China, ranking with the deities of Heaven and Earth. Today his teachings are the basis for education and all civil service examinations in China

Ancient religions; Brahmanism-

The Hindu Faith

Early India was animistic with numerous gods. As Aryan invaders came to India they built up an elaborate ritual. This ritual they wrote into the Vedas, or wise saying, and tried to maintain order by establishment of the caste system. Originally there were four castes, the Brahmans, or priests, the warriors, the merchants and traders, and the Sudra, or miscellaneous groups. The fifth, established later, was the Untouchables. Only the first remained pure while the others broke into many sects and sub-sects The Brahmans became rich and powerful and through their ritual were able to control even the gods.

As the religion moved south, all the old gods followed except the great triad, Brahma, Vishnu and Shiva. Probably it was Shiva who provided the source of the Yoga mysticism which so interests some moderns. It seems certain that a spiritual trance does occur. The older philosophical explanation of the trance was that it was a glance of the Great Beyond. Modern psychologists explain it more likely a sublimation of sexual desire.

Liberation and the absorption into the It, or Nirvana-state of mind rather than a physical state, the ultimate good. Nirvana; a state of mind to be gained by complete annihilation of the ego. Death was not a release but merely an interval between periods of conscious existence. Depending on the form of life dictated the reincarnation life either in a better or worse form than the previous life.

Hinduism today is the strongest religion in India with over three hundred million devotees. Its single most revered note is caste, established by law in the code of Manu. All adore the Brahminic gods. All accept the prescribed rituals, venerate the cow, observe rules of caste in marriage, sharing of foods, and all accept the orthodoxy of Brahminic scriptures.

In the Bhagavad-Gita we find: He who does his work for my (Vishnu's) sake, who is wholly devoted to me, who is free from attachments to earthly things, who is without hate of any being, he enters into me.

Hinduism began, by most historian's calculations, around 3000 B.C. making it the oldest major belief system. Bhagavad-gita,"the ultimate guide to self-realization" is its most cherished of Hindu 'scriptures', a 700verse in poetic form, written by Krishna, the major god of Hinduism, and the god of compassion and love. Krishna was believed to be the eighth reincarnation of the Hindu God, Vishnu (the godhead of the Hindu trinity of deities).

Hinduism outdates the beginning of Buddhism by twenty-five centuries, and after three thousand years remains India's major religion. Buddha was somewhat like a Martin Luther, in that he wanted to reform aging Hinduism. However, his movement while flourishing for some seven hundred years, slowly lost its power, especially among the downtrodden, and today is somewhat strong in only three small countries.

The following are the closing words of the Gita's chapter 10, typical of many God claims of Krishna in these writings. This poem was delivered to an Indian Prince over a period.

"I am alike for all! I know not hate, I know not favor! What is made is mine! But them that worship Me with love, I love; They are in me and I in them.

If one of evil life turn in his thoughts straightly to Me, count him amidst the good; He that hath the highway chosen; he shall grow righteous ere long; he shall gain the peace which changes not. Thou Prince of India! Be certain that none can perish, trusting me! O Pritha's Son! Whoso will turn to me, though they be born from the very womb of Sin, woman or man; sprung of the Vaisya's caste or lowly disregarded Sudra, -all plant foot on the highest path; how then the holy Brahmans and my Royal Saints?

Ah! Ye who into this ill world are come-fleeting and false-set your faith fast on me! Fix heart and thought on me! Adore Me! Bring offerings to Me! Make Me prostrations! Make Me your supreme joy! and, undivided, unto My rest your spirits shall be guided."

ANCIENT RELIGIOUS BELIEFS IN THE AMERICAS

In the western hemisphere, we find primitive religions still flourishing in the sixteenth century, when the white man came.

Religion of the Aztecs

Most highly developed were the Aztecs of Mexico, with a polytheism and a highly organized and numerous priestly hierarchy. By the time the white man came to America, the Aztec religion was largely controlled by the priesthood.

Evidence reveals there were two sources of their beliefs. Originally, they were a monotheistic group and their

Supreme being remains in the later polytheistic pantheon as an omniscient and omnipresent deity. But by the sixteenth century there were many gods-thirteen principal deities and approximately two hundred lesser gods. Their mythology tells of four distinct eras in the past, at the end of each, man was destroyed and later reestablished on a new and higher plain.

Temples were numerous, one city of three hundred thousand population reporting over six hundreds of them. They provided homes fir the numerous priests when they were in attendance on the deity. The temples were the largest buildings in the city, built like the pyramids.

At the top was a tall sanctuary with a sacrificial altar in front between two fire alters. On the latter, the priests maintained perpetual fires. So numerous were the temples that at night some cities were well lighted by these alter fires. Each temple was supported by gifts. Any funds remaining after expenses were donated to charity, thus preventing the priesthood from becoming too rich.

The chief deity became the sun and there is no evidence of general human sacrifice to this god, Tezcatlepoca. To him there was a single annual sacrifice of one human victim, chosen a year in advance. This practice dates to the fourteenth century. During the year the victim was treated with highest of honors as to one representative of the highest deity. On the day appointed six priests led a procession of the whole community through the streets to the alter. With one surgical swipe of the knife the victim's heart was then ripped from the naked breast and held up as an offering to the Sun, then cast down at the feet of the deity. The body was then prepared as a fast for all and regarded as a sacrament, not degrading to the partakers of it. Probably, cannibalism was practiced in centuries before.

Later, human sacrifices became more common with the

war god Huitzilolotchli, the patron god of the state. He is represented in the temples with a fantastic image with a prominent sacrificial stone for he demanded human sacrifices in large numbers. Most of his victims were prisoners of war. We find the Aztecs had a treaty with a friendly and peaceful neighboring tribe to meet annually in a certain place for a battle with the sole purpose of obtaining captives on both sides for sacrificial purposes.

There are many parallels with Christian teaching. In their ritual of naming children, we find a very similar act to Christian baptism. The lips and breast of the infant were sprinkled with water, and "God" was implored to take away the sin given the child before the foundation of the world.

Religion of the Incas

Another great religious society or nation in America was the Incas of Peru, so called from the family name of their rulers. Probably in ancient times they had been nature worshiping cannibals with war a chief pastime, but by the time the European explorers came in the sixteenth century they had developed a very high civilization with an architecture at least equal of anything in the old world.

According to their legends, the Great sun father sent two of his sons to teach the arts of civilization to his people. The center of their nation was Lake Titicaca. The temple of the Sun was the most magnificent, with the riches and the most elaborate buildings in the Americas, rivaling anything in the ancient world.

The two sons married, and their decedents were the Incas, who ruled by divine right because of their divine origin. To preserve and maintain the divinity line of every Inca married his eldest sister and the descendants 4 of this marriage succeeded to the throne. Unlimited polygamy was permitted the Inca. The progeny of the Inca's unions seems to have been numerous in some cases upwards of three hundred children, according to certain accounts. All the children held official rank in all phases of Inca society, including chief priest, judge, and army leader.

The perpetual fife ritual was one of the oldest pagan religious rites and was the Incas' major religious rite. They regenerated their altar fires by friction every fifty second year in their greatest festival celebration. The Romans maintained a perpetual fife in the temple of Vesta. Perpetual religious fires have survived to the modern times in such as a lighted candle before the images of the saints.

The Incas were free thinkers. They noted that even the Great Sun was regulated in its course, and therefore must not be the supreme authority. From this fact sprang the belief in a supernatural god superior to the sun. Rites such as infant baptism and confession of sins were practiced. Infant sacrifice was replaced by blood being drawn but the life spared (a practice that could be compared to that of circumcision of males). The Incas had a Holy Communion ritual using a sacred bread called sancu sprinkled with the blood of a sacrificial sheep.

The people were oppressed with severe laws and tyrannous taxes. The nobles, (Inca families) were exempt. Yet, material well-being was at a very high level, with cities marked by clean, well-lighted streets, and the Incas surpassed all Europeans except the Romans in the arts, road building, law administration, architecture, and agriculture. In general, we may say that they reached the highest civilization of primitive people in the Western Hemisphere.

Chapter 2

Faith of the Hebrews -Judaism

The early Hebrews were similar in every respect to their neighbors. They believed in the same supernatural beings, in holy trees, holy stones, and other similar fetishes. Since early Hebrews had no conception of the universe it was impossible for them to formulate the idea of a supreme infinite god. Yahveh, or Jahvey, later Jehovah, like all primitive gods, was a spiritual being, rather more easily aroused to wrath than most of the early deities. He was not the loving father pictured by David in later times, but a jealous god -a demanding deity who forced his followers to give up all other gods and even to forsake worship of ancestors. In the early period, he was neither omnipotent, omniscient nor omnipotent.

Each village had its place of worship and idols have been found from time to time. Yahveh revealed himself and the future in dreams and revelations. As in early times, sacrifice was a gift to either beg the deity to show favor or to express gratitude for favors already bestowed. As in other early aniministic religions, there were tabus of abstinence, cleanliness, clean and unclean foods, curses and blessings. The blessing of the father was especially esteemed to the eldest son. Witness the account of Jacob and Esau. Sin against Jahvey and crime against the tribe were one and the same. Ignorance of the law was no excuse. One man's sin might bring retribution to the whole tribe. Later individual punishment was meted out.

Abraham is the first truly historical figure. He left Ur of Chaldea around 2000 B.C. after a long period of nomadic peregrination in the Arabian desert and Egypt, where they eventually settled and where they were later enslaved. About 1200 B.C. their greatest historian, Moses, raised in pharaoh's palace led them out of bondage. After a period of nomadic wandering and travail, the Hebrews finally settled in Palestine, the promised land of the old testament. During this time the first five books of that which later would be the Old Testament were written.

Shortly after the settlement in Palestine, about 1000 B.C., the Hebrews organized themselves into the kingdom of Israel. Three kings ruled successfully over the kingdom; Saul, David and Solomon. After Solomon's reign the kingdom broke in twain, Israel with its capital in Samaria and Judah with its capital in Jerusalem.

The change in history brought about a corresponding change in religion. Israel was a wealthy nation of town dwellers who accepted the customs and gods of the Canaanites. Judah, the southern nation, was a poor nation of farmers and herdsmen who clung to the ancient Yahveh. Baal thus became the god of the northern kingdom and the rich, Yahveh, the support of the poor.

The prophets belonged to this period and supported their god vociferously, sometimes violently. Elijah proclaimed war between Yahveh and Baal calling down punishment on those who followed baal and the easy ways of town life. The Israelite royal family and the Canaanite priests were slain, but with no lasting religious revival-Yahveh remained a war-god belonging exclusively to the Hebrews.

Also, in this period belongs a body of writings, the "good times" when the land flowed with "milk and honey." Acquainted with the Egyptian social reformers and

24

philosophers, Hebrew writers incorporated their philosophies in defense of the poor and defenseless into their own writings.

With the prophets Amos, Hosea and the second Isaiah (750 B.C.) religion changed from a ceremonial ritual to a way of life. Fear of god became love of god and religion became a social force. Amos made an historical leap as he wrote down his teachings to ensure their preservation. In the early seventh century B.C., Isaiah was the prophet of the period and he began to proclaim Yahveh as a universal god, omnipotent and omnipresent.

Judah was invaded and the Hebrews there taken into Babylonian captivity by Nebuchadnezzar in 586 B.C. The captivity added much to their philosophy and theology. Babylonian law was parallel with much of the Talmud and influenced many of the Hebrew laws. Jex Talionis, the eye for an eye, a tooth for a tooth law came from the Babylonians. The sun hymn and psalm 104 have remarkable parallels.

After Cyrus restored the Hebrews to Palestine, the temple was built at Jerusalem. Here the law, the psalms and the prophets remained as separate holy books until the time of Christ when they were organized into the Hebrew bible or as better known, the Old Testament.

Later the Hebrew state church was overrun by Alexander the great and then by the romans, who ruled during the time of Christ. About 135 A.D. came the final diaspora, or dispersal and since that time the Jews have been a religious group without a countly.

Judaism is a reasonable and moderate belief. The central truth of its teaching is that the final aim of religion, the summum bonum is morality. To the Jews right conduct in everyday life is more important than right belief. According to the Talmud, every good man is assured of heaven. And the heathen who observes moral law is being equal to the high priest. Judaism is truly a catholic belief: "thou shall love thy neighbor as thyself."

An eleventh century Hebrew writer sums up the teaching thus: "speak the truth; be modest; live on the coarsest fare rather than being dependent on others. Shun evil companions, be not like flies that swarm in foul places. Rejoice not when thine enemy falls; be not both witness and judge; avoid anger, the heritage of fools."

Aristotle's theory of the "golden mean" can be seen in the Talmud also. "The law may be likened to two roads, one of fire, the other of snow. To follow the one is to perish by fire, the other of snow. To follow the other is to perish by fire; to follow the other is to die in the cold. The middle path alone is safe.

Variants within Judaism

The three major variants or streams of Judaism are orthodox Judaism, conservative Judaism and reform Judaism (often called 'liberal' or 'progressive'). In the united states, most Jews are affiliated with reform temples.

Orthodox Judaism

Orthodox Judaism is distinguished by its maintenance of the traditional forms of worship in the Hebrew language, and in the traditional observances as prescribed by the Torah. Men and women sit separately in orthodox synagogues and women do not participate in some of the rituals.

Orthodox Judaism is not administered by any central authority. Synagogues are established by groups of Jews who raise their own funds and construct their own buildings. The congregation usually elects a volunteer board of management, which employs rabbis and other official; a system not unlike many independent protestant churches. The result is that each synagogue may represent a distinctive ideological variety of Orthodoxly and therefore attracts congregants who share that approach and background. Some attracted are connected to the religious Zionist movement, and a number are simply gatherings of like-minded people in houses or rooms.

The 'Ultra-Orthodox'

The long black coats, flowing beards and picturesque hats with variations indicate religious movements. Some of these movements are characterized as 'Chassidism', a movement in search for ecstasy in prayer, an interest in medieval mysticism and an emphasis on the possible imminence of a Messianic era. (One can readily see the parallelism in today's Pentecostalism) Chassidism was a way of infusing joy and hope into life. Many traditionalists felt it stressed the heart at the expense of the mind.

Conservative Judaism

Conservative Judaism fosters the practice of traditional Judaism while embracing modernity. Developed during the twentieth century in the United States, it comes midway between Orthodox and Reform, intellectually liberal in matters of belief, but conservative in matters of religious practice. It represents a belief that Judaism is constantly evolving to meet the contemporary needs of the Jewish people. Four interesting departures from Orthodox standards: men and women sit together, and women participate fully in the synagogue services, prayers and rituals; in their 1960 assembly, they agreed to pe1mit the use of electrical appliances on the Sabbath and drive to synagogue by car. In 1985 they permitted the ordination of women Rabbis

Progressive Judaism

In the early nineteenth century, a new element entered the Jewish world; Progressive, Reform or Liberal Judaism. Liberal Judaism migrated to North America from German culture and the philosophy of the 18th century Enlightenment. The 'Science of Judaism', reflected the developing understanding of evolution, history and Biblical scholarship. Most recently the American Reform movement platform emphasized a distinction between the divinity of the "moral laws and statutes" and laws of ritual observance which "no longer impress us with the character of Divine institutions."

In 1999, a Statement emphasized the study of the Hebrew language and the sacred texts, commitment to Israel, and the full equality of women and the acceptance of sexual orientation. Progressive-services: The English Language is used in parts of the service, which often features a mixed choir. Women rabbis may officiate. The term 'temple' is used by more 'Progressive' congregations, while the term, 'Synagogue' is used most in naming of the Orthodox and Conservative congregations' meeting facilities.

All three major groups use a traditional congregational prayer with a few variations;

Orthodox "…and brings a redeemer to their {Patriarchs) children's children…. Savior…the Shield of Abraham."

Conservative; "…and will send a redeemer (repeat above) because of your loving nature." …several Old

Testament women are added in some congregations .... "

Progressive; "...and brings a redeemer to their.... Savior... (many women's names included), ... shield of Abraham and the helper of Sarah."

All three refer to a *redeemer* in approximately the same language, the only consistent reference and terminology in the three prayers. This seemingly refers to their long expected Jewish Messiah and his unending reign as King from Jerusalem.

Eschatology

The State of Israel and its place in evangelical eschatology. in the current political climate, we hear and read of many evangelical Pastors and others placing U.S. support of Israel as a litmus test for supporting any major candidate. Why is this? Let's begin with a statement of Jewish belief as it relates to Kingdom theology

For centuries before Christ's advent and to this day religious Jews place as one of their most sacred faith issues the expectation of an everlasting earthly Kingdom with their yet to come Messiah as King with his throne in Jerusalem; One who embodies the attributes of the conquering warrior David.

Jesus' disciples were Jews schooled in that belief. On more than one occasion they inquired of Jesus as to when he would set up or "come into His Kingdom" and ostensibly route the Roman armies. They believed earthly Jerusalem would be his throne city. Their ' great warrior' King would put down all threats. There would be a utopia of never ending peace and prosperity.

Some years ago, I invited a friend, a local Jewish Rabbi to address our church's combined-adult classes to share his and Jewish beliefs. I had someone ask him what he believed about life beyond the grave, heaven and the Kingdom of God. His answer certainly caught many by surprise." I believe the Kingdom/heaven will be an everlasting earthly economic utopia". He didn't offer what might be his afterlife existence.

However, in a visit with our local newspaper editor and friend who was also Jewish, I asked him what he believed would happen to him after death. After some thought, he said as a person he would no longer exist and his life after death would be his gifts of influence, teaching and example that would live on in his children. He added that in many matters relating to Jewish teaching, "no two Jews believe alike"

Jesus as their Messiah? No, but they in large believe him to have been a prophet, great teacher and a holy man. But he could not have qualified in one of many senses as their military leader/king. "If My kingdom were of this world, my servants would fight, so that I should not be delivered to the Jews; but now my kingdom is not from here". To thwart the growing threat of his becoming a competing Messiah, they had him put down. His continued talk of the Kingdom of God being "not of this world" would result in having to defend their own earthly utopian concept and further enrage the occupying Romans.

A BRIEF EARLY HISTORY OF PALESTINE.

The west holds a view of something like this about Palestinians and the Jews:

The Jewish people, having suffered tremendous persecution, needed a haven-a national home land.

Their Zionist leaders had chosen the "uninhabited" land of Palestine. Supposedly, the surrounding Arab nations were naturally antagonistic and jealous that the Jewish settlers had turned a wasteland into a paradise. They had risen unprovoked against the Jews, forcing them to fight a valiant War of Independence in 1948. However, many Palestinian accounts of personal experiences and historical records tell a different story, a terribly ironic twist of history in which the persecuted became the persecutor.

The following: a brief ***Palestinian position***

In 1897, a conference convened in Basle, Switzerland, to "lay a foundation stone of the house which was to shelter the Jewish Nation." Leader: Theodor Herzl, Father of a political movement called Zionism, had hopes to rescue the 'downtrodden, humiliated' Jews from the big city ghettoes. (Even though Jews had become more prosperous in their newly chosen worldwide habitats, than any other immigrant people)

Palestinian leaders called Zionism a blasphemy and felt the Zionists, non-religious Jews, believed that Zionism was the only Messiah Israel would ever have. Both orthodox and the more pragmatic Jews believed Zionism would feed anti-Semitism since it underscored the long-criticized "exclusiveness" of the Jewish people.

Palestinians in the 1900s were downtrodden people struggling and suffering under the Turkish Ottoman Empire. After WW I the Empire crumbled, and the winds of freedom were felt for the first time in centuries. The League of Nations proposed a plan that would help "subject peoples" Mandate system.

The Mandate system was instituted by the United Nations in the early 20th century to administer non-self-governing territories. The mandatory power, appointed by an international body, was to consider the mandatory territory a temporary trust and see to the wellbeing and advancement of its population.

In July 1922, the League of Nations entrusted Great

Briton with the Mandate for Palestine. Recognizing "the historical connection of the Jewish people with Palestine." Great Briton was called upon to facilitate establishment of a Jewish national home in Palestine-Eretz Israel (land of Israel). Shortly afterwards in September 1922, the League of Nations and Great Briton decided that the provisions for setting up a Jewish national home would not apply to the area east of the Jordan River, which constituted three-fourths of the territory included in the Mandate and which eventually became the Hashemite Kingdom of Jordan.

The British Mandate authorities granted the Jewish and Arab communities the right to run their internal affairs; thus, the Yishuv established the Elected Assembly and the National Council. The economy expanded, a Hebrew education network was organized and cultural life flourished.

The Mandatory government failed in maintaining the letter and the spirit of the Mandate, and under Arab pressure, it withdrew from its commitment, especially with respect to immigration and land acquisition. The White papers of1930 and 1939 restricted immigration and acquisition of land by the Jews. Later immigration was limited by the1930 and 1939 White Papers, and land acquisition by Jews was severely restricted by the 1040 Land Transfer Regulations.

After the United Nations General Assembly adopted the resolution to partition Palestine on November 29, 1947, Britain announced the termination of its mandate over Palestine, to take effect on May 15, 1948. On May 14, 1948, the State of Israel was proclaimed.

Zionism

The British saw the opportunity, and helped oust the

Turks' in return, they set up a Mandate government in Palestine. Desperate, the Palestinian leaders agreed.

Then came a secretive agreement involving the British, French and Russians to divide the Middle East into "spheres of Influence", governed not be the people of Palestine but by an international administration. They protested to no avail.

In 1917 the Zionists aligned themselves with Great Britain's Christian Restorationists, a group that believed they might bring to pass, by manipulating world events and reestablishing the nation of Israel,

By the 1930s with the influx of European settlers rising like a flood tide, the Palestinians' pleas to Britain and the world fell on deaf ears. Then in 1936, the leaders called for a general strike, on lasting 6 months. The powerful trade union, Histraduth, established by the Zionists and led by David Ben Gurion, teff01ized Jewish shop and factory owners who dared hire Palestinians. Women were attacked for buying from Palestinian merchants; fields and vineyards were vandalized and finally stolen.

By 1938 the Zionists had world sympathy behind them. Why?

18. Western nations were fixated on horror stories coming out of Nazi Germany.

19. Appalled by insane hatred of the Jews by Hitler and rightly the Jews needed somewhere to escape from the madman. Soon after, the Zionists controlled all news emanating from Palestine. The protests of 1936-1938 were renamed "The Arab Rebellion". Some have suggested that in any other country being overtaken by a foreign force, the protesters would have been called Freedom Fighters, but here they were called, "terrorists and "guerillas". Hence the name," Palestinian te1Torists" was ingrained in the western mind.

Following WWII, the Zionist shifted their power push from a weaker Britain to the White House. In America a strong lobby of new Zionists supporters had emerged. Roosevelt, with great compassion opted for a plan whereby the Jews could be offered free passage to any free nation. His emissary, M01ris Ernst was sent to sound out international opinion. He was sneered at and attacked as a traitor by Zionists who by then had raised $46M to lobby their own plan.

After Roosevelt's death, the lobbyists pressured the new president Truman, claiming admission to Palestine was "the only hope of survival" for the Jewish people. Could this have been true when millions of Jews were sheltered and protected by free nations during and after the war? In fact, Jewish people moved freely in their societies without discrimination. Truman's response to the pressure: "I'm sorry gentlemen, but I have to answer to hundreds of thousands of those who are anxious for the success of Zionism; I do not have hundreds of thousands of Arabs among my constituents."

Worship in Egypt and the fertile crescent

In Egypt we find a curios mixture of ancestor worship, animal and nature worship, totemism, sun worship, and a high type of monotheistic belief. Each dynasty as it came to power tended to set up its own family deity as the chief god of the country, adding to it the attributes of other main deities. Two main religions of the earlier period seem to have been animal worship and ancestral worship. Tokenism was a natural growth in animal worship. Its symbols took on the bodies of humans with the heads of animals. Greatest; Amon, the ram.

The two principle deities were re, the sun-god and Osiris, god of the Nile river. The most sacred text was the book of the dead, a collection of magic formulae and spells, making possible the passage of the soul from earth to the judgment hall of Osiris. Every spring the life of Osiris was re-enacted in a stirring passion play, dating back to the eighteenth or nineteenth century before Christ. The play is the earliest record of drama.

As belief in immortality grew, so did the desire for morality, and religion for the first time ceased to be a matter of form and ritual and became a matter if justice, force and a way of life.

Religious leaders came and went over the period before Moses. Most were able, for a short time, to establish new faiths, usually backed by law and then force. The people under these leaders were commanded to accept these new religions and give up their old polytheistic beliefs.

However, each time a 'progressive leader' passed, the old priesthood gained control again and restored their beliefs and rituals. Much art, architecture and massive buildings were destroyed under the priesthood. Nevertheless, a tendency toward monotheism remained in Egypt.

The Fertile Crescent

The people of the fertile crescent may be divided into three main groups: Babylonians, Hittite and Assyrians. The Babylonians have left much religious literature. With them the worship of the moon seems to have preceded sun worship. Among the chief deities was Assur, god of ever reviving vegetation. The well-known Roman deities; Jupiter, Venus, Saturn, Mars and Mercury were first

Babylonian gods. The Babylonians gave god names to the seven days of the week, and the nomenclature has survived to our day-the names however, changed to roman and Teutonic forms.

Among the later Babylonians, the goddess Ishtar became the chief deity with Marduk, a secondary national deity. Ishtar later became a sex dealing, life breeding spirit, the goddess of love and marriage, probably the first of the great earth mother goddesses. Aphrodite and Venus possessed the attributes of Ishtar.

In Babylon it was common for every woman to wait at least once in the courts of the temple of Ishtar and lie for an hour with a stranger to overcome sterility. The priests-who willingly supplied the place of the 'stranger'-became rich with the price of harlotry. By the time of Hammurabi, the temples had amassed great wealth and large possessions. In many towns the temple was the center of business life, trading, and banking with interest as high as 20% per annum. The priests had many cults, each with its own work to do-to offer sacrifice, to care for the idol, to fructify barren women, to foretell the future and to sing praise hymns.

The Assyrians took over most of the legends and symbols of the Babylonians, but always retained Assur, after whom they were named, as chief god. Their religion carried no belief in judgment after death, thus having little effect on their conduct and tending to make them a fierce and inhumane tribe.

The Phallic Cults

The history of primitive religions would not be complete without some brief mention of the sex religions, or phallic cults. They seem to have originated with the worship of the earth mother in the fertile crescent who became recognized in different countries as Ishtar, Isis, Aphrodite or Venus.

The chief male counterparts of these deities were Baal, Tammuz, Marduk, Adonis and Mercury. All followers of these phallic religions worshiped with licentious rites. Their most famous god was the Hindu Siva. He with Vishnu and Brahma made up the main triad of these peoples. Today in India there are about three million followers of Siva, known as the lingayat.

The phallic religions are important for their contribution to the culture side of civilization. In the time of the Greeks, one of their rites was the Dionysian festival with its tragos, or goat song. This was the origin and the forerunner of that great branch of literature and entertainment known as the drama.

5th Century Sophists;
Challenging Traditional Religion

The Sophists of Greece, dating to the 5th century, B.C. have sometimes been characterized by their attacks on the traditional religious beliefs of the Greeks. It is true that more than one sophist seems to have faced prosecution for impiety as did Socrates also. Protagoras wrote concerning the gods. "I cannot know either that they exist or that they do not exist nor what they are like in form." Critias went further when he supposed that the gods were deliberately invented to inspire fear in the evildoer. It seems the tendency of much Sophistic thought was to reject the traditional doctrines about the gods in their attempt to explain the phenominoral world from within itself while excluding all principles or entities not discernable in phenomena.

William F. Lawhead, in his book, "The Modem Sophists" writes; "One of the realities of Athenian life that Socrates lamented the most was the prominence of the Sophists. The Sophists prided themselves in being able to make the weaker argument the strongest. Socrates decried the Sophists because they did not recognize the difference between faith and opinion, believing everything was relative. Modem lawyers in a very literal sense are arguers for hire. Early Sophists were not concerned with truth but only with winning the argument."

In observing moral conduct in present day societal expressions, it may be helpful to study the influence of philosophies such as those propagated by the Greek Sophists and their philosophical decedents. To the Sophists, the laws of nature were regarded not as generalized descriptions of what happens in the natural world but rather as norms that people ought to follow but are free to ignore. This philosophy advocated free reign for the passions. In response, Plato argued that human nature, if it is to be fulfilled, requires organization and restraint in the license given to the desires of particular aspects of it: otherwise the interest of the whole will be frustrated.

Two Important Observations:

First, the Sophists' agnostic attitudes toward the Olympian deities were probably at one with most pre-Socratic philosophers of the 6th and 5th centuries and with most thinking people of their time. It is probably misleading to regard them as revolutionary in their religious beliefs. Second, one of the most distinctive Sophistic tenants was that virtues can be taught and that teaching of a high intellectual caliber could produce success both for the individual and for governments, offering profound influence upon the subsequent history of education.

Though scattered throughout Greece, the Sophists mostly gathered in Athens where they found the greatest demand for what they had to offer; instruction to young men on acquiring the 'tools' of success. They were the 'higher education' elite of their period.

The cult spread quickly throughout Europe with its promise of immortality. The Mithraists became Christians easily, for whereas Mithras was always subtle into a mysterious abstraction, Christ was literally humanized; and in religion the concrete always carries more force than the abstract.

Hence, the Islamic State of El SHAM, (also ISIS*- meaning the area LEFT or the region centered in Damascus) or The Islamic State of Iraq and Syria

Mythology

There were three ancient peoples that developed the most complete mythologies; The Greeks, the Romans and the northern Teutons, or Norsemen. The early Greeks thought of spirits or gods in all-natural objects. Each had a limited sheer of influence. One could ordinarily gain favor or avoid displeasure by making a simple gift. This later became a blood sacrifice or the smoke of a burnt offering.

*Isis; was an Egyptian God. The modem term, ISIS has its roots with both geographic and political/religious connotations.
human beings, there was little moral significance being attached to religion. At death it was believed that most men passed to a gloomy, dark, dreary spirit world. One of their great warriors is reported to have said that it would be better to be least in the kingdom of men than to be the

greatest in the kingdom of the dead.

For many centuries in Greece, the Olympic pantheon held sway. The home of the gods was Mount Olympus, and hence the name. Zeus was the greatest of the gods, the father of mankind. The Greeks had over 100 gods with names, beginning with Achilles and ending with Zeus. Later the Romans adopted most of their gods and subsequently gave most new Roman names. Each had its own area of rule.

In this writer's college classes, one was a study of Greek philosophy and architecture which was entitled" Greek Adjustment." To this day, the title is still confusing: Was the study intended to adjust to the Greeks or to the students?

To gain salvation the Greeks developed several mystery cults. By this time the Greeks had awareness of immortality, and membership in these cults spoke to this belief.

In Rome, the earliest religion was centered in the family. Later, the Romans developed a state religion taking over the family gods and most of the old Greek gods but giving the latter new Latin names. The Roman gods were never as immoral or sensual as were the Greek Olympic gods, but neither were they as puritanical as the Hebrew Yahveh. The Roman religion was clean but cold.

The early Teutons and the Norse peoples were found to be both animistic and anthropomorphic.

They thought all things, animate and inanimate, possessed spirits like their own. At least three ideas of future life were extant among these peoples.

First, their heroes were thought to undergo transmigration, spending eternity in Valhalla.

Second, the soul remained in the grave.

Third, the soul fell into the great abyss of the goddess

Hela. If possessed by virtues, it might bypass the demons to a happier place. The evildoer, if not punished in this life, would gain fit recompense hereafter. The supernatural beings fell into two groups-the giants and the gods. The giants were evil. They believed that there would be one last great fight with the giants when the end of the world would come.

Mithraism

In the 5th Century with a promise of better things to come, and increasing doubts about the ancient gods, there was an influx of new 'mystery' religions. In Rome, the Earth Mother Attis or ISIS cult had many followers-traces of Isis worship are found as far west as the Seine River in France. This was the period when the "oracles' flourished, especially the one at Delphi.

One of the earliest forms was belief in a future life celebrated in Chthonian worship. The Chthonian believed that man felt the same wants, pains and pleasures in the future life as in the present; that he had the same property rights; that he had the same need for wife, cook, horse, tools, etc. The main difference was the power to do harm. As a man was under the protection of his gods 'at home,' it is easy to understand the fear of banishment shown by the ancients. Their religion touched not heart or conscience, and that explains their moral code. Acts which seem to us political were to them religious. Every war was a 'holy war' because it was against people with different gods. There was no moral obligation to captives, who might be sold, or enslaved, or slain. Even the Roman census was for religious purposes, to ensure that all attended the lustration of atonement for previous shortcomings of the state.

Many cults arose in Greece and Rome. involving myths and legends of the birth, adventures, death, and resurrection of a youth representative of the sun, life, or light. Another group was centered on the prolific Earth Mother, and of these the Isis cult was most far flung. The Romans would have made a cult of Jesus if they could, and they did add much of the ritual of their most popular cult, Mithraism, to their Christianity.

The Mithraism cult was introduced to Rome about the middle of the first century and flourished through the second and third centuries, becoming a serious threat and rival of Christianity in the whole Western world. Originally a Persian deity, Mithras was supposed to have been born of a virgin, the birth being witnessed by only a few shepherds. Ahura Mazda had made him the deity of truth and light, a sun god equal in majesty to the Supreme Being himself, and the chief supporter in the fight against Ahriman, the spirit of evil. His life reached its climax in the great bullfight, a struggle against a great bull allegorically representing the forces of darkness. By slaying the bull and letting his blood, Mithras symbolically fructified the earth.

Since Mithras was a sun-god, Sunday was automatically sacred to him-the "Lord's Day" --long before Christ. On December 25th, just after the winter solstice, there were elaborate rituals and celebrations. Bells were rung, hymns were sung, candles lit, gifts given, sacraments of bread and water administered to the initiate. Between December 25 and the spring Equinox came the mystical forty days' search for Osiris, which later was the origin for Christian Lent.

Initiation into the Mithraic mystery was an elaborate ritual probably lasting twelve days. The initiation was no simple process and sometimes involved painful trials of fire, water, hunger, thirst, cold, scourging, bleeding, branding, and mock menace of death. There seems to be no historical evidence for the tales of fearfulness in these rites or for any licentiousness being involved.

Chapter 3

BEGINNINGS OF CHRISTIANITY

Into an era of the great philosophers, ancient gods and Oriental mystery religions, came Christianity with all the advantages and most of the attributes of the Eastern religions, and a higher ethic than any of them. Christianity had in common with the mystery cults that man could "get right with God." There was a savior-God who had become a man to teach mankind a way of life, who had died, who had been resurrected and through whom those who had faith in him would be saved.

In some cases, pagan rituals, whole or in part, were adapted to the new religion. From the east came conventional architecture, the Mosaic arrangements of figures, the use of the halo and incense (it was due, in great part, to the use of these Eastern practices that the Christian Church eventually broke in two-the Roman Church and the Greek Church.)

From Judaism, Christianity adopted the idea of the Fatherhood of God and the brotherhood of man, and the idea of Christian love, mercy, and justice. From the Greeks came many philosophical ideas-"the Word," "the Logos," "the Godhead." To the Greek words had the same attributes as gods, for they could be used repeatedly without wearing out, but rather growing in strength and meaning with use. The Roman contribution was late in coming, but not less important-Romans gave organization.

The historicity of Jesus: born in Bethlehem, about 4 B.C.

The first thirty years of Jesus's life was spent in Nazareth at the carpenter's bench of Joseph; hence the term "Nazarene" which is often applied to him. Modern archeology lends some support to the belief that he spent part of this time in travel and study in the Far East. After this period and upon the imprisonment of John the Baptist he set out to preach and prophecy. This was the time of Tiberius and there were two ways for the Hebrews to show their defiance to the grinding of the Roman heel. One was by arms, the other by faith. To this group advocating the latter Jesus belonged.

Much of his teaching was based on the Rabbinical writings, both ancient and modern, but he brought a new form of metaphors and parables to his preaching. His oft statement, "It has been said of old, BUT I say unto you," was used to then trump many Jewish laws. He spoke as one having authority rather than an interpreter. His eloquence attracted a great following and although he never claimed to be the Jewish Messiah, he was hailed by many as such. He preached of the Kingdom of God presently in believers, which angered the Jews who could only accept a kingdom doctrine with a future earthly Kingdom and their Messiah reigning from Jerusalem in a rebuilt temple.

Feeling free from custom and law, he evoked the ire of the higher Jewish classes-the scribes, Pharisees and Sadducees.

Jesus's teaching began with doing "the will of God," to follow the Golden Rule in all relations with their fellows, to be merciful and compassionate to all. His teaching in some cases reflected old Jewish homilies and had a tremendous appeal to the common man-"Come unto me all yet who are weak, and heavy laden and I will give you rest" I gave dignity of life to the lowest people. Will power to do good, application of common sense to everyday problems and neighborliness were the keynotes of his teaching. To his seeker's question, "what must I do to inherit eternal life?" His, "Ye must be born again" answer laid foundationally the believers hope of eternal life beyond death. Rather than a Jewish works-oriented pursuit, Jesus taught a God/believer eternal relationship initiated and anchored by faith and rebirth.

He was a man of uncomely open mind as witnessed by some of his lectures: "Render unto Caesar the things that are Caesars, and unto God, the things that are God's." ... "Let him who is without sin among you cast the first stone at her." His teaching was aimed at spiritual rather than physical things; character building rather than power or wealth; at evaluating man by what he is rather than by what he has. It was a faith which was intended to be a way of life, not a ritual shell.

On a thumped-up charge of political conspiracy, the Jewish leaders had Jesus tried before the Roman governor, Pontius Pilate. Although Pilate found the evidence against him inadequate, the Jews desired his end so much that he was condemned and crucified. Following his execution, his disciples dispersed, but the cross was destined to become the symbol of love rather than disgrace.

It remained for Saul, a Pharisee, a Roman-Jewish tentmaker of Tarsus, to 'rescue' Christianity from the always present oblivion of other Messianic cults and give it world meaning. At first Saul had persecuted the Nazarenes, but later was converted. Through his own experience he knew that the old Judaic law was insufficient, and he came to think of Jesus as a personal Redeemer, Savior, or Lord, through whom he and all mankind could attain personal salvation.

Jesus always remained a Jew, but Saul, the Jew, became Paul, the Christian founder. Paul was a statesman, builder and organizer. His 'religion' took root in Antioch, where probably the contemptuous term "Christian" was first

46

used. Christian missionaries then started small Christian communities in cities where want and poverty were greatest, and from there the faith spread. Paul's letters (in Greek) to those communities provide much of the material for the New Testament.

In addition to Paul's letters, the most important part of the New Testament is made up of the four gospels. Due to the dating of the writings some historians believe that these accounts were not penned by these disciples although they bare their names. Many believe a biography of Jesus in his own language, Aramaic, was written, and the four gospels were drawn from this and the original was lost. The gospels were written in Greek a generation or two after Christ-the earliest one -Mark, about the year 65, and the latest, John about 100.

Christianity had an advantage over mystery religions because it offered a real human being to worship, and it had real gospel as evidence. Although it adopted some pagan forms it never became pagan in spirit but retained its Jewish puritism and always avoided sensuality. If it had to fight for existence it remained strong and pure, but as soon as it gained permanence it became softer and weaker and schisms appeared.

By the end of the second century Christianity had a larger following than any cult. The Roman government persecuted the Christians on three levels. First, the Romans held them to be unpatriotic because they foretold the fall of the Empire, would not sacrifice to the Emperor, and would not perform military service. Secondly, they maintained that the Christians were antisocial because they would not participate in the festivals. Thirdly, the Romans thought them immoral because families broke up when some became Christians.

For a time in the third century, every citizen had to carry

a libellus, a certificate showing that he had sacrificed to the Emperor which had to be produced on demand. During this period persecution was most severe because the Christians would not conform.

In the fourth century, emperors like Constantine were beginning to realize the support they might get from this 'sect' to bolster their crumbling Empire. In 313 the Edict of Milan was passed giving Christianity equality with emperor worship and other religions. Clergy were exempt from taxes, churches were built at public expense and the church was given its own courts. Sunday was made a legal holiday, In the middle of the fifth century paganism was suppressed by the Theodosian Code, 438, and all citizens were required to be members of the orthodox Church.

From that point the growth spread rapidly among the barbarian Germanic tribes on the outskirts of the Empire. The Holy Catholic Church, forerunner of the Holy Roman Empire grew quickly. As it became more powerful, heresy became punishable, even by death.

The Church was lowly in origin, its greatest appeal to the poor and downtrodden and grew rapidly in the cities. While the pagan beliefs focused on this life, Christianity focused on the future life, making the burden of life lighter for such people. The Medieval stage in church devolvement is marked by numerous hermits and anchorites and by withdrawal from the world and by asceticism or self-inflicted punishment.

Higher Greek learning and rut were brought into the church by men like Augustine, Constantine and Gregory I. Church architecture took on the form of Roman art with ornately decorated interiors with mosaics, images, stained glass, and vessels of precious metals. The divine power of the Church was attested to by the miracles of the saints. Monks began collections of manuscripts and began circulating them to other church libraries-a practice which help preserve much Greek and Latin culture and literature through the Dark Ages. To avoid heresies and interpretations in the Church, Constantine had the Nicene Creed, an official statement of belief promulgated in 325. The creed is still used in many churches today, although the more common Creeds include the Athanasian Creed. the Apostles Creed and the Westminster Confession of Faith.

In the early church there was little organization because the Christians looked for a speedy return of Christ. Church organization began with a presbyter or priest. Later as the church expanded the work demanded full time and the priests became clergy as distinguished from the laity.

Later the chief priest of the city became a bishop, and the Bishop in the Chief city became the archbishop, now an organization like the Roman Empire. Five of the archbishops became very influential and took the title of "patriarch." Four of the five were from the east while one was from the west-Rome.

The Roman patriarchate gradually achieved greater influence. This was due to several causes-the Roman Church was thought to have been founded by St. Peter who had been commissioned by Christ. Also, the Empire of Rome was the fountain head of much missionary endeavor. Pope Leo I, 440-461, had the Emperor declare the Bishop of Rome supreme head of the Christian Church in445. The Bishop of Constantinople was set over the Eastern Church a few years later. Gregory The Great, Pope 590-604, took over the government of Rome, which was retained by the Papacy for twelve centuries. At first all higher Church leaders were called Pope, but it was not until the time of Gregory VII in the eleventh century that the title "Pope" was reserved to the Roman Bishop.

The Confessions of St Augustine, one of the earliest books written by Augustine was a guide for all Christians who feel themselves being tempted. In his City of God, he outlined an invisible catholic Christian state, scarcely distinguishable from the organized Church. This book ended all intellectual liberty on the part of the believer, who was admonished to submit without reservation to the Church and the Pope

BEGINNINGS OF CHRISTIANITY PART 2

Under Justinian, state support was taken from the philosophical universities and given to the Church, with the result that some magnificent buildings were built. Perhaps the most imposing is the great Church of St. Sophia in Constantinople, built about 532-537 at the cost of eighteen tons of gold plus the work of ten thousand laborers over the period of five years. The dome of St. Sophia is vast-one hundred eighty-three feat high-and probably the most imposing interior still extant from early times. It was seized by the Turks when they took Constantinople and has been used as a mosque since 1453. The great Christian mosaics were covered with large plaques or whitewashed. In recent times permission has been granted to clean the mosaics, with a revelation of magnificent art made of fine coloring in glass and marble cubes inlaid with gold and silver.

When the Empire began to break, the Church first separated itself from secular control, and then seized temporal as well as spiritual authority as a rich and powerful Church-State; it claimed the right to govern all true Christians. It taught that the Church was supreme rather than subject to king and emperor. The Pope was supreme judge, administrator, law giver and interpreter of scripture as well as possessor of the keys to heaven itself. His legate took president over all Church hierarchy. For violations; excommunication, its most potent penalty. Canon Law, a new code, was developed and applied to all trials of the clergy, and to all offences against the Church such as heresy, atheism, adultery, and sacrilege. Immense revenues accrued from church property, tithes and bequests.

The Church became the center of social life. It directed all education, dispensed all charity, controlled all the universities and book publishers and controlled all hospitals. All matters pertaining to family life, marriage divorce, birth and death records, succession and wills-were in its hands.

The church maintained the idea that it controlled the entrance to heaven, which made the threat of excommunication which would act as a bar to the entrance to heaven.

As the Church advanced in power and importance, so the sacramental rituals increased in number, variety and elaboration. A sacrament was defined as a sign of inward grace. Over time the number of sacraments, recognized by the Church, was reduced to seven:

1. Baptism of the newborn child
2. Confirmation
3. The Eucharist
4. Confession
5. Extreme Unction
6. Holy orders
7. Marriage

This growth resulted in a weakened leadership, as much of its clergy was underpaid, and lacked sufficient education. Greedy Bishops with plural benefices, absentee clergy, charging fees for administering of sacraments added to the evils of the Church and detracted from its prestige. Out of this heresy arose. One of the earliest was:

1. Arianism: God alone was God. This controversy resulted in the first ecumenical Church conference at Nicaea in 325, and As the Church grew, it spread to all of Europe the Nicene, or Athanasian Creed created.

2. Gnosticism: Belief in two deities, the Supreme Being and a lesser Spirit of evil. They flatly denied the human body of Christ and proclaimed him a phantom spirit who came from the Supreme Being to give enlightenment to mankind. To answer this heresy, the Apostle's Creed was promulgated. Much later to further bolster the orthodox faith, a body of scripture was compiled, which became the New Testament. Also, later, as another means to combat this heresy, some Bishops began to claim "Apostolic Succession" to their seats, that is, began to assert that they had received their authority directly from the Apostles with special directions and interpretations to be passed on directly to their successors.

3. Catharism: Believed in the dualism of God, that there was a universe of two principles, either spirit or matter, or good and evil. Their God of evil was identified as Jehovah of the old Testament, connected with pestilence, was and matter, where as their God of Good was revealed in the New Testament as entirely beneficent and connected with brotherly love, charity and the spirit. They declared that all tales of the virgin birth, crucifixion, and resurrection

were impossibilities since Christ was purely spirit. They abolished such refinements as, baptism of children, mass, veneration of saints, the cross, and the doctrine of transubstantiation. Catharism divided their followers into two classes, the perfect and the believers: Any believer could become perfect by laying on of hands and by swearing to refrain from moneymaking, shedding of blood, use of profanity, to abstain from flesh, milk, cheese, and eggs, and to live henceforth a celebrate life. Very few Catharses were "perfect". Every believer was required to become perfected at least in the hour of death. Suicide was permissible after the perfecting ceremony (the Consolamentum)

Catharism was popular because of its high ethical teachings, because of its attacks on the wealth of the Church and because of its diatribes against the morality of the clergy. By the end of the twelfth century the Church was so concerned that it called on various European rulers to stamp out this heresy. The attempt met with so little success that in 1209 the Pope declared a Crusade against the Aborigines. This too failed and resulted in driving the movement underground.

Early Church-Monasteries and Missionaries

Monasticism arose early in the Christian community. Benedict of Nursia, 480-543, was the earliest organizer for those living the life of asceticism and puritanism. He drew up a 'tulle' or constitution for the conduct of monks and monasteries. The monastic life continued to appeal to those believing and practicing a hermit life style. Vows of poverty and celibacy were required and enforced. Frequent prayer and meditation were required. There were seven regular daily periods of devotion, lasting about twenty minutes each.

The Monasteries themselves followed a regular plan. A great portion of the monk's time was spent in the 'cloister' where he did his writings, reading, studying and teaching. All monks slept in the common dormitory. Only in the warming house was a fire permitted. Only in that room was the rule of ·silence or solemnity relaxed.

The contribution of the monasteries to Medieval and modem times is enormous. The most recognized contribution is the preservation of books, manuscripts and numerous translations of them during the Dark Ages. Jerome, as a monk, gave the Vulgate version of the Bible still used in the Roman Catholic Church today. The roster of their great men is numberless; Martin Luther, Erasmus, Roger Bacon, Thomas Aquinas, Gregory, and Boniface to mention only a few. Not least important was their missionary endeavor-their aim being not only conversion to Christianity, but subjection to Papal authority.

As early as the thirteenth century, there were two orders recognized by the Pope. St. Francis of Assisi, 1181-1226, was the son of a merchant and lived a fast life as a youth. Narrowing escaping death, introspection led him to life as a hermit. In 1208 he had a revelation to go and preach. His message was one of poverty. In 1210 he and his followers' official designation was "Friars Minor," better known as the Franciscans. The second group recognized was the Dominicans. While the Franciscans appealed to the lower classes, the Dominicans developed a following among the upper class.

A third great missionary order was the Jesuits, the founder; Ignatius Loyola and Francis Xavier formulated "the principles of the Order of the society of Jesus, or Jesuits" emphasizing discipline along military lines for teachers, preachers and confessors. Membership increased rapidly. The order was officially recognized by the Church in 1540. The order performed great missionary endeavors in Europe, Asia, and America and is still a flourishing Roman Catholic mission effort.

The Russians were converted to Christianity by missionaries from Constantinople in the eighth century. When Constantinople fell to the Turks, the Tsars felt themselves divinely appointed successors to the patriarchate and undertook to defend all true Christians who accepted the Greek Orthodox faith. Peter the Great, brought the Church completely under government control. Russia with rights to protect the Sultan's Christian subjects, seized the excuse to expand toward the monasteries and missions and continued southeast. Thus, did Russia set the pattern for imperialism to follow in the wake of missions.

From the seventeenth century on, we find the various churches organizing missions. Dutch and English Protestant missions were established in the East Indies in 1602. In 1622 a Roman Catholic Missionary Board was established to train missionaries for the work and to teach languages. In 1695 the Church of England formed the Society for the Promotion of Christian Knowledge. During the eighteenth century the Baptists and Methodists established mission fields. The American Board of Missions of Foreign Missions was organized in the United States in 1810. In the Twentieth century, Bible Societies have sprung up to translate and distribute the Scriptures in many languages. Today we accept missionary endeavor as an integral part of religious work.

While not motivated by missionary vision, the most marked religious endeavor in the eleventh through the thirteenth centuries was the Crusading movement. By the eleventh century Jerusalem had become the Holy City of the Christian world. Pilgrimages from the Christian world created a wealthy city. With magnificent shrines, churches and monasteries to visit (and pay fees) it was one of the grandest destinations of the time. All this ended when the whole area was taken by the Seljuk Turks.

The Byzantine emperor, Alexius, appealed to Pope Urban II for aid, and this appeal led to the First Crusade ("War of the Cross") against the Seljuks. The Turks, who had recently been converted to Mohammedanism pursued their new found faith with a zeal that led them to begin persecuting the Christian Pilgrims, This further ignited the stirring to take up arms against the Turks. Many inducements, for this crusade and the seven that followed, were held out to those would participate; remission of sins, indulgences, the hope of plunder and 'great adventure.' The audience responded, "God wills it."

The goal was to 'redeem' Constantinople, but the effort failed. On the way home, the crusaders conquered Antioch and Jerusalem in 1098, to be held for nearly a century until Saladin finally regained it in 1187. Jerusalem then became head of a feudal organization rather than a Church-state as the Pope had hoped.

The fourth Crusade launched in 1202, was directed against Constantinople rather than the Turks. The Crusaders succeeded in capturing the Brigantine capital and installing one of their own as ruler. An attempt was made to place the Eastern Church under the authority of Rome, but this effort designed to unite the church by force was doomed to failure.

The result of the Crusades was widespread and far reaching. The advance of the Turks was stayed. The papacy had both. The Crusading Movement continued won and lost-lost in power but gained in prestige and wealth through missions to the East.

One evil result was the development of the sale of indulgences because all crusaders were grated absolution. Culture and science were introduced on an ever-increasing scale. Man began to look upward and forward. The world was getting ready for the metamorphosis from medieval to modem times.

Chapter 4

Mohammed, "the praised one"

Arabia was destined to produce one of the world's great religions, a belief which was to attract over four hundred million followers. Early Arabia was divided into three sections, without any political unity. Most were nomads. Tribal warfare was common, but each year there was a four-month period when no fighting was allowed. During these sacred months pilgrims were allowed free passage across the desert so they could pay their respects at the holy shrine of the Kabba in Mecca. The Kabba still stands now a Mohammedan shrine. In the Kabba was a most highly venerated black stone of meteoric origin. This shrine was the single most unifying influence among the Arabians before Mohammed.

Many deities were worshiped, and much paganism was found, interspersed with Jewish and Christian communities. A single clan, the Bana Hashim, had risen to prominence. Into this, 570 A.D., was born Ubu'l Kassim, later to be known as Mohammed, "the Praised One," just as Gautama later became known as Buddha. Although he had no schooling, contacts made with Eastern religions would influence him greatly.

In appearance, he was not remarkable, with large extremities, head, hands and feet. He was well thought of by his neighbors, and was known for his wisdom, and pertinence of conversation. Unable to read or write, he yet had a keen insight into the psychology of human nature. From middle life on he suffered from nervous disorders which caused lividity, foaming at the mouth, fits of unconsciousness, fever and fierce headaches.

In the employ of a rich widow, young Mohammed rose

to become the manager of her trading interests, doing so well that eventually she married him, although she was much older then he, the marriage was a success. He remained faithful to her until her death, and always spoke with reverence of her memory, holding her in much more esteem than any of his later wives. Known as a good father and stepfather, he was not yet an outstanding man in his community.

This first marriage made him financially independent. In his travels he became exposed to the monotheism of the Jews and Christians, and ideas of asceticism from the latter. From one of his lonely vigils in the desert he returned with the firm conviction that the angel, Gabriel had appeared to him in a vision and summoned him as a prophet who was to proclaim the doctrine of a single universal god, Allah Akbar ("God is Great") He began to prophecy of a Day of Judgment, with a future of rewards and punishments. Islam is largely based on Christianity but should not be judged as an offshoot of Christianity. At first, he had few converts, only thirteen in three years including Khadija and his close friends. When he began to preach openly in Mecca, he invoked the ire of the priests who were the keepers of the idols. His own tribe, the Koreish, gave his followers the despised title of Muslims, or Moslems, meaning "traitors" but the name was to survive with the new meaning of "the reconciled ones," or "those who submit to Allah."

ISLAM-

In July 622, an attempt was made to assassinate Mohammed in spite of the law against bloodshed in the Holy City, Mecca. Some converts had made it to the city of Yathrib, and so Mohammed and the Moslems moved to that town. The flight took on the name of "Hegira" and marks the beginning of the Mohammedan era. The first work was to build a mosque for prayer. Hoping to win Jewish converts, Mohammed at first gave the order to face Jerusalem for prayers but failing in his purpose he ordered all to face Mecca. With little success in winning converts, he resorted to a well-established form of religious trickery-the addition of some pagan rituals-with considerable success.

Because he needed funds, and partly because his followers were not schooled in agriculture as were the natives of Yathrib, he organized fighting bands to raid caravans. Having no ties with the older religions, he sent the fighters out even in the peace months. That started Arabia's Holy War. Mohammed's whole movement took on the character of religious militarism. He made the Moslems fanatic fighters by teaching that admission to paradise was assured to all of those fighting in the cause of Allah. After his first success, the name of Yathrib was changed to Medina, "The City of the Prophet." By 631, all Arabia, including Mecca, had been conquered. He returned to Mecca as the Holy City and died there the following year. He brought new unity to the Arabs, which was to result in their becoming a world power.

The desert tribes now fired with religious zeal spread Islam from India to Spain, Egypt, Syria, Asia Minor, and North Africa. Constantinople fell before the advance of the Moslem Empire. The victory over the Turks at Tours, France, in 732 by Charles Martel, was all that prevented their conquest of Europe. How different might have been the history of western Europe had the Moslems conquered!

The Caliphs, or "Successors," unified this great new empire. Their function was fourfold-religious, militaly, judicial, and political. In 762 a new capital was set up at Bagdad, which became the center of learning and science. The teachings of Mohammed were here compiled to make the Koran.

, The Koran: "the thing to be read", was entirely the work of Mohammed, being dictated to scribes. Supposed to be of divine revelation sent from heaven at various times over a long period, it is contradictory in parts. It does set a high standard of law and practice. The contents of the Koran, as assembled in Bagdad are divided into three sections. In the first, are found laws and precepts for the regulation of religious and civil life. The second, contains histories and fables which closely parallel the Old Testament narratives. The third section contains admonitions and threats of Hell for all unbelievers. Here the duties of industry, temperance, and justice are outlined. All its twenty-nine chapters are required reading for all Moslems.

Islam had been defined as "Judaism plus Christianity minus the teaching of St. Paul." Mohammed's revelations were produced from trances like those of a modern spiritualist medium. The reality of a Day of Judgment with an afterlife of rewards and punishments was emphasized. Both heaven and hell were sensual and were pictured as we would expect desert people to picture them.

Hell was a gulf of fire, where the sinner could neither escape nor perish, but must suffer continuous beating with maces. Heaven, reserved for followers of the Koran and those slain in battle, was a beautiful garden of bliss. Here the soul of the believer, dressed in green robes, lolled on green cushions, enjoying forgiveness, fruit, wine with no headache in it, and service by beautiful maidens (described as "black-eyed, well rounded of hip, but of modest withal"). At the day of judgment, the souls of all sinners were to be annihilated, the souls of unbelievers to be cast into hell and burned and tormented forever.

Polygamy provided for a surplus of women and served as a check on prostitution and a protection against illegitimacy, for the child of a concubine slave inherited equally with other children. To the Moslems, adultery is a very serious offence, and is punishable for both sexes equally, by one hundred lashes delivered publicly. Once women were segregated, but that rule along with equal punishment for sexes rule, has been modified; one in favor of women, the latter in favor of men.

The Moslem has five definite religious duties:

1. Daily recitation of his creed; "There is no God but Allah, and Mohammed is his prophet."

2. Prayer; after proper absolutions, five times daily, before and after sunset, at the day's close, before sunrise, and just after noon-facing Mecca, kneeling, with forehead to the ground.

3. Charity; at least one-fortieth of income, to carry on religious warfare, to maintain the mosques, and to spread Islam. (A number do give a tenth (tithe) of their income)

4. Fasting; throughout the month of Ramadan (compare Christian Lent)

5. Pilgrimage; at least once during his lifetime to Mecca where the Moslem must circle the Kaaba seven times, each time kissing the sacred black stone.

We must not lose Mohammed the prophet in looking at Mohammed the history-maker and organizer. He left a code of ethics which was a tremendous step forward for his time. Islam became a great civilizing force. It stopped infanticide of girls, restricted slavery, and imposed a kindlier treatment of slaves. It opposed drunkenness and gambling, almost ended tribal feuds, and limited free polygamy. It extended religious tolerance to both Judaism and Christianity. (a tolerance which has greatly waned in recent years) Among the Moslems today we find no taverns, no brothels, no gaming houses, no profanity. Modem Islam has seventy-two sects with some animosity among them, but nothing like the bitterness and intolerance found among many Christian sects. Islam is followed by one-fifth of the world's population and is continually making new converts.

SHIITES AND SUNNI

The differences between Sunni and Shiite Muslims are predominately political and stem from disagreements after the death of Mohammed. Most elemental tenets of faith remain agreed upon by both branches. Sunni Muslims make up more than 85% of the world's Muslim population. Both groups simply identify themselves as Muslims rather than members of one of the two parties. Dating back to the death of Mohammed, a disagreement arose as to whom should take over leadership in the Muslim nation. The Shiite Muslims believed the leadership should have been passed down to Mohammed's son-in-law. Historically Shiites have not recognized the authority of elected Muslim officials, instead choosing to follow imams, whom they believe have been ordained by the Prophet Mohammed.

These imams are said to be sinless and infallible by the Shiites, who enshrine these men and perform pilgrimages to their tombs in hopes of divine intercession.

Sunni Muslims counter that leadership is not by birthright, but by earning the people's trust, with no intercession of saints or deifying of imams.

Islam religion; music and art

Music in the Islamic world is to express and encapsulate the most important concept of the Qur'an: tawhid, or "unity with God."

There are various devices that Muslims use to express tawhid, but in sum these characteristics can be described as forms of abstraction: "Since tawhid teaches that God cannot be identified with any object or being from nature, He cannot be musically associated with sounds that arouse psychological or kinesthetic respondences to beings, events, objects, or ideas within nature" (al Farouk, 1986).

Thus, Islamic music must be nonprogrammatic and must not create events that would evoke or express extra-musical ideas that are associated with human emotions, human problems, or earthly musical occurrences: "We refer to the saying of the Prophet in which he condemned artists who 'ape' the creation of God: in their afterlife they will be ordered to give life to their works and will suffer from their incapacity to do so" (Burckhardt, 1987).

Such abstraction can also be readily perceived in Islamic art-"arabesque" art, for example, which never depicts images of humans, animals or the natural world, but instead focuses solely on the creation of patterns. The point of Islamic music and art is to avoid focus on worldly concerns, which are of no value and only distracts man from focus on God:" Islamic art corroborates a void with abstract forms, instead of ensnaring the mind and dragging it into some imaginary world, thus detaching the consciousness from the inward 'idols.' In other words, man without images of himself can remain more pure and uninhibited from contemplating God.

(1000-1200) High middle ages

Expansion; Monastic and Papal Reform

Demographic expansion:

Christianity was spreading throughout Western Europe with ecclesiastical allegiance placed in Rome. In Eastern European countries, principally Russia, Christianity was being widely accepted and for political reasons pledged their dependence on the Constantinople patriarch.

The health of the religious institution:

The ninth century Papacy had reached a low point of spiritual decline. In general, for the following two centuries, the papal office became a prize over which Rome's noble clans fought. Popes were drawn mostly from aristocratic leadership. It was a continuing conflict between Germany and Italy over the right to appoint the Popes. The Roman nobility in later years usually won out.

The Episcopal Level:

Discipline and learning receded as clerics were obliged to become part of feudal relations. Kings and more powerful feudal lords began to appoint bishops and protect churches. Lay control was often the result of these liaisons. Priests who back-slid into clerical marriage, were often incorporated into clan control. These priests focused less on the religious than in using church property to support their family and feudal lords. The monasteries were affected in the same way when the abbots (managers of the monasteries), also became agents of the powerful lords. At times the feudal lords acted as titular abbots. This opened the way to simony, the auctioning off church posts to the highest and most often least qualified bidder.

Relationships: Clerical and Feudal

Through the tenth and into the eleventh century some in church service were appalled by practices such as clerical marriages, simony, and general subservience to secular feudal leaders. In Burgundy, earnest monastics were able to convince William the Pious of Aquitaine to found the CLUNY monastery in 910. It was endowed liberally from the start with relatively few strings attached, so it would not be beholden to feudal lords.

These gifts would not be in return for feudal services but would be recompensed by the monk's prayers. Idle time was addressed by the founders by instituting heavy schedules of communal liturgical prayer services, fieldwork and manuscript reproduction. This allowed a high level of sustainable piety and discipline throughout this period.

The Cluny-based monasteries proliferated throughout France and western Europe. The original Cluny compound had 300 monks, in addition to 150,000 dependencies. Alumni of Cluny went on to ascend even to the papacy. One mark of this era was the church's effort to curtail violence in feudal society. Councils proclaimed the TRUCE OF GOD whereby fighting on religious holidays was proscribed, as well as attacks on noncombatants. It is not clear as to the success of such proclamations, but it did establish the Church's position on the high moral ground.

Later came the Reforming popes.

They would articulate the idea of a papal monarchy entitled to temporal powers for the sake of spiritual betterment of Europe. In the process they would come into direct conflict with the German patrons of the clerical reform movement. Between 1046 and 1049, Henry III of Germany had appointed a string of Popes, his last, Pope Leo IX (1049-54) was tremendously significant.

High Middle Ages...Monastic reformers (1090-1153)

In addition to the Cluny monastery and Order, the following were major Orders of the period.
1. St Bernard of Clairvaux (1090-1153)

His Order was called both Cistercian and Trappist. St. Bernard wore white symbolizing purity which was the thrust of his SPIRITUAL revival of the church message which framed the religious tone of the twelfth century. Joined the Cistercian Order in 1113; a Charismatic Recruiter Plea: Return to simplicity. His Abbeys: Beautiful and productive sites Chosen to form a new monastery, Abby of Clairvaux (Later to be converted to a prison by Napoleon) Influenced the Rule for The Knights Templar One of the most fervent preachers of the Middle Ages

His message to a school of theological students:

"If you desire to know what is inside leave behind the bodies that you brought into the world, only souls are allowed "

2. St. Bruno (1030-1101)

His Order was called Carthusian. Pursued eremitical life; embraced poverty, manual labor, prayer, and transcribing manuscripts. Followed the Rule of St.

RENEWAL within the movement; Monasticism

In the thirteenth century a new form of monasticism emerged called the mendicant orders, placing a premium on quiet devotions. The mendicants, were so called because they begged for their subsistence. Their monks became known as the Friars, the name derived from the Latin word for brother. Two important orders: Franciscans, and the Dominicans. The Franciscans were founded as an order to win back the heretics in Southern France. The Dominicans became connected with the Inquisition, that famous effort to win back heretics by torture and persecution. The Franciscans sought to win men by the example of good deeds, while the Dominicans stressed learning and logic in their approach. Both however, contributed greatly to the Scholastic movement of this period. They did not often agree in matters of doctrine, but both were missionary minded to the extent that whatever growth occurred in the church, much could be attributed to these two groups, even to this day.

Scholasticism

In addition to great missionary growth this period witnessed a great revival of learning. This movement is often referred to as Scholasticism, an effort to support the faith by reason. These Scholastics tended to study religion/theology from the viewpoint of philosophy rather than from the Bible. Their writers relied heavily on the writings of Plato and Aristotle.

One leading spokesmen was Anselm (1 033-1109), a native of Italy who later became the Archbishop of

Canterbury. His efforts to combine faith and reason was summed up in this statement, "I believe in order that I might understand." For him, faith was the basis of knowledge. In contrast to Anselm's approach was that of Abelard (1079-1142) who lectured in theology at the University of Paris. His motto; "I understand in order that I might believe." Regarding atonement, he held that Christ died to set an example, and to exert a moral influence upon man, a view akin to modem liberal theology. He is also known for his attitude toward Church Fathers as reflected in his book, "Yes and No," where he showed that on too many occasions the Fathers contradicted themselves.

The greatest of all Scholastics was Thomas Aquinas (1225-1274). Born of a noble Italian family, he was educated in Monte Casino and the University of Naples before he became a Dominican monk. In his greatest work, Summa Theologica (a summary of Theology) he used reason to argue the existence of God. Although he used reason to argue the point, Thomas felt it was necessary to go to scriptures to learn of God's loving concern for man.

Thomas's greatness lay, not only that he was an innovator, but that he was successful in synthesizing faith and reason. He believed that God was the author of both reason and revelation, and there was no conflict between the two. Thomas's thinking and reasoning was so systematic that it has held great sway with scholars both within and without the Roman Catholic Church ever since. His position was not without critics, who argued that truth in doctrines could not be demonstrated by reason. William of Occam, a Franciscan, came after him denying that dogma could be demonstrated by rational arguments. He argued that the basic tenants of Christianity must be accepted by faith, thus abandoning any hope of reconciling the wisdom of God and the wisdom of man. After that time, Scholasticism began to decline.

Life, worship and religion of the late Middle Ages.

Change could best describe the church of this period. A new culture had emerged in the west. The classical heritage of Greece and Rome was eventually eroded by the invading barbarians from the north and east. The church had been somewhat effective in taming some of the wild barbarian passions yet had been affected in the process. To appreciate this new cultural one need but compare the apostle Peter to one of his "successors"-Pope Innocent III for example. Or compare the simple faith and worship of the first century Christians with the superstition-laden worship of the Middle Ages.

Compare the two New Testaments ordinances, Baptism and The Lord's Supper, which had grown from two to seven, and now called Sacraments: defined by the Roman Church Catechism as; "efficacious signs of grace whereby divine life is dispensed". The present seven sacraments: baptism, confilmation, penance, the Eucharist, extreme unction, marriage, and ordination

Infant baptism had become a universal practice of the church. It was believed that an infant dying un-baptized could not, because of the taint of original sin, enjoy the presence of God. The mode of baptism; immersion or affusion (pouring). Private confession to a priest had become widespread practice as was the performance of good deeds commanded by the priest, who had the power to forgive sins.

Note: Not only is the "remission of sins" granted by the priest in the private confessional booth but also in the corporate worship/mass where all may be granted this forgiveness. Among today's Protestant churches, at least one, the Lutheran Church, Missouri Synod, corporately practices Pastoral granted forgiveness. The fourth Lateran Council required every Christian to attend confession at least once a year. As a part of the system, the practice of indulgences had grown. By doing certain good deeds one could receive an indulgence that would remove from him the temporal penalty of sins. Urban II, for instance, granted a plenary indulgence to any who went on the first crusade. By the end of the Middle Ages it was popularly believed that the living could obtain indulgences that would supposedly help them in Purgatory.

The Eucharist:

At the heart of public worship was the Eucharist, or the Mass. By this period the cup had been withdrawn from the laity, who got only the bread. Also, the Fourth Lateran Council declared that the doctrine of Transubstantiation to be the official dogma of the church. This doctrine declared that the bread and wine became the actual body and blood of Christ in the ceremony of the Mass. The mass was said in Latin, and since fewer and fewer of the laity could understand Latin, the ceremony tended to lose its original significance.

Satan and Demons:

To persons in the Middle Ages the unseen was very real. Satan and his cohorts were considered the source of many evils. Since Christ had overcome Satan, the cross and other symbols were used extensively as fetishes to ward off the evil spirits. Since the 'saints' had also triumphed over evil, they were revered. The Virgin Mary was, and is, especially honored. In a later chapter, The Mary Cult will be discussed. Mary and the Saints were thought to be already in the presence of God, and thus to pray through them was to get special hearing from God.

Pilgrimages were popular. Travel was quite hazardous in the Middle Ages. Yet there was a steady stream of pilgrims making their way to Rome and for the more hearty to the Holy Land. Relics became treasures sought after. Clothing, bones, and personal effects became objects of veneration. Traffic in relics became big business.

Architecture: Scattered across most of western Europe are great Romanesque and Gothic cathedrals. These building tower over their surroundings giving evidence of religion's place in people's lives.

Note: Preaching one Sunday morning years ago, this writer, somewhat casually, spoke a critical note concerning how the poor people (Catholic) in a particular Mexican village were sacrificing exceedingly, even going without food in some cases, to build a vely imposing and magnificent church building which dwarfed its poor surrounding and far exceeded in costs and structure any other structures in the village where most of the inhabitants were in need of a helping hand. That Sunday we were hosting our missionary to that village and area. After the service as the parishioners were leaving, and as Pastor I was shaking hands, I noticed, standing back, a rather small and frail lady whom I had never seen before and seemingly waiting to talk to me. To my embarrassment, she smilingly spoke that she was visiting today and would soon return to her home in that village where she "counted it a blessing and high privilege to have personally sacrificed to finally complete their wonderful church that God had given them." To this day, I have endeavored to be very careful in not criticizing publicly the motives and even the actions of a person that could be the symbol/s of a deeply held faith. In this study, however, in examining religious history and assessing modem religious challenges, I may stumble somewhat with occasional critical bias.

The Middle Ages was a period of contradictions. The church in many ways had departed from the simple church of the first century. Yet despite the corruption the church was able to provide a light, flickering but steady, as it led men to keep reaching higher.

High Middle Ages in England

From the end of the 16th century there were also Congregationalists or Independents. They believed that every congregation had a right to run its own affairs without any outside interference. Charles II (1660-1685) was not particularly religious but as far as he had any religion he secretly leaned to Roman Catholicism.

Meanwhile parliament was determined to crack down on the many independent churches that had sprung up during the interregnum (the period between 1649 and 1660 when England was without a king) and make Anglicanism the state religion again.

They passed a series of acts called the Clarendon code, a series of laws to persecute non-conformists (Protestants who did not belong to the Church of England). The Corporation Act of 1661 said that all officials in towns must be members of the Church of England.

The Act of Uniformity 1662 said that all clergy must use the Book of Common Prayer. About 2,000 clergy who disagreed resigned. Furthermore, the Conventicle Act of 1664 forbade unauthorized religious meetings of more than five people unless they were all of the same household.

Finally, the Five Mile Act of 1665 forbade non-Anglican ministers to come within 5 miles of incorporated towns. (Towns with a mayor and corporation). However, these measures did not stop the non-conformists' meeting or preaching.

When Charles II died in 1685 he was followed by James II, who was openly Catholic. James II promptly alienated the people by appointing Catholics to powerful and important positions. In 1687 he went further and issued a Declaration of Indulgence suspending all laws against Catholics and Protestant non-Anglicans.

Worse, in June 1688 James had a son. The people of England were willing to tolerate James if he did not have a Catholic heir. However, his son would certainly be brought up a Catholic and would, of course, succeed his father.

James II was deposed in 1688. Afterwards the Bill of Rights (1689) said that no Catholic could become king or queen. No king could marry a Catholic.

Parliament also passed the Toleration Act in 1689. Non-conformists were allowed their own places of worship and their own teachers and preachers. However, they could not hold government positions or attend university.

In the early 17th century king and parliament clashed over the issue of religion. In the 17th century religion was far more important than it is today. It was a vital part of everyday life. Furthermore, there was no toleration in matters of religion. By law everybody was supposed to belong to the Church of England (though in practice there were many Roman Catholics especially in the Northwest).

In 1633 William Laud was made Archbishop of

Canterbury. He was strongly opposed to the Puritans and King Charles I supported him wholeheartedly. Laud was determined to suppress the Puritans and he sent commissioners into almost every parish to make sure the local churches came into line. Furthermore, the Puritans had their own preachers called lecturers. These men were independent of the Church of England. Laud tried to put a stop to these preachers -with some success.

Most of all Laud emphasized the ceremony and decoration in churches. These measures were strongly opposed by the Puritans. They feared it was the Thin edge of the wedge' and Catholicism would eventually be restored in England. In 1642 came civil war between king and parliament. The war ended in 1646 and Charles I was executed in 1649.

In the 16th century everybody was supposed to belong to the Church of England. However, in the 17th century independent churches were formed. The first Baptist Church in England began meeting in 1612.

Chapter 5

The Protestant Revolt

Many were the contributing factors in the Roman Church's failure to appeal to Europe's growing educated population. One such was that the Church, being inherently conservative, did much to hamper scientific research. Another was the resistance to the papal yoke. By the end of the Middle ages, a split had appeared between the north and south, and Protestantism was a fait accompli. England had always been recalcitrant and irked by the Pope's authority.

Under Henry VIII the real rift came. He asked the Pope to grant him a divorce from his first wife, Catherine, claiming she had been the first wife of his older brother and that such a marriage with a brother's widow was forbidden. The Pope refused claiming the marriage had taken place under special dispensation. Henry tried to bring the Pope to his way of thinking by cutting off papal revenue and then by an Act of Parliament which forbade the appeal of any case outside the realm. An English Church court then granted the annulment.

In 1534, Henry went a step further by passing the Act of Supremacy. He thus became the Supreme Head of the Church in England. Those who would not recognize his leadership were convicted of treason. The next move against the Roman Church was to seize the properties of monasteries and abbeys. It must be understood Henry was not a Protestant but was Catholic and simply took the Pope's authority to himself in his own kingdom.

Under Edward VI the confiscation and destruction of stained glass and images was completed. Edward also seized the funds to pay for Masses for the Dead, and the right of appointment of bishops. He issued a new Prayer Book, containing forty-two articles of faith. Under Mary, there was a nominal return to allegiance to the Pope, and we find severe persecution of heretics, with nearly three hundred executions.

Elizabeth came to the throne as the first Protestant sovereign, having Parliament establish the Church of England with the sovereign as its head. The Roman Catholic system of government was retained with archbishops, bishops, etc. Elizabeth did not hesitate to use persecution as a weapon, and it is estimated that more than two-hundred were executed during her reign.

The belief of the Church of England was set forth in a revised set of thirty-nine Articles and a new Book of Common Prayer containing a prescribed order of services was authorized. The Mass was abolished, and fines were imposed for attendance at Mass or for nonattendance at Anglican services. It was the time that many Roman Catholics, and many Protestants Dissenters -Baptists, Quakers and Methodists, sought refuge and escape in America. Many of these groups settled primarily in Pennsylvania and Maryland.

Protestantism first appeared in France in the fifteenth century along with the Renaissance. A renewed interest in the classics led Lefevre, 1450-1537, to make a translation of the Bible into French directly from the Greek. He preached justification through faith long before Luther appeared in Germany. By the middle of the sixteenth century, persecution of the Protestants was rampant in France, and many leaders like John Calvin fled to Switzerland. Despite persecution, the Protestants, or Huguenots as they were called, increased in number and formed a strong political party under such leaders as Henry of Navarre and Coligny. In 1562 they gained permission by the Decree of

Toleration to hold daylight meeting outside of towns. The treacherous premeditated Massacre of St Bartholomew's Day, August 23, 1572, is one of the blackest pages of Church history. Catherine of Medici, the queen mother, persuaded the king to kill the Huguenots while in Paris to attend the wedding celebration of Henry of Navarre and the king's sister. Estimates of the killings sometimes total as high as fifty thousand, but probably one half of that would be more nearly correct.

The next trouble was the so-called War of the Three Henrys. This turned out fortunately for the Huguenots. HenryIII had Henry of Guise assassinated. The latter's followers then murdered the king, and Henry of Navarre automatically succeeded to the throne. For him to take the crown, he had to become a Catholic, but his famous jest, "So fair a kingdom is surely worth a Mass," is an indication of how serious his conversion was. He issued the Edict of Nantes in 1598, the first strong move toward toleration, which would remain in effect for nearly a century. Under the Edict the Calvinists were permitted to hold meetings anywhere except in Paris and certain specific towns. They were also granted equality of political rights.

In Germany and Austria, Protestantism took root. Luther, of whom more later, began the revolt here. Early in the sixteenth century, the Confession of Augsburg outlined the path the Reformation was to take. The Peace of Augsburg was an arrangement whereby the princes were given freedom of choice between Protestantism and Catholicism for the areas under their control. So important was the reform movement that in 1545 an ecumenical council-the Council of Trent-was called, which sat for nearly twenty years. Its object was to chiefly condemn the Protestant belief, but some of the reforms helped to strengthen the Church from within. The seven Sacraments were ratified, the Vulgate version of the Bible was accepted as authoritative, and the supremacy of the Pope was recognized. It was this council that first instituted the "Index of Prohibited Books," a system of censorship still used by the Roman Catholic Church. The clergy was subjected to several reforms, their duty being emphasized. Protestantism continued to grow.

The treaty of Westphalia in 1648 at the end of the Thirty Years' War reiterated the Peace of Augsburg giving the rulers the free choice of religion. In Austria, Joseph II in the late eighteenth century followed a pattern set by Henry III in England. He confiscated the monasteries, using the property for schools and charity. He forbade sending money to Rome, took to himself the appointment of bishops, abolished the marriage Sacrament, making marriage a civil ceremony by license. Frederick the Great was the first truly enlightened monarch in religious matters: but later, recognizing their importance as allies against socialism, he repealed the laws against the clergy and came to a cordial concordat with the Pope.

Early church -Waldensians

Another important heretical group were the Waldensians, who wished not to break away from the Church but to reform it by a return to poverty and simplicity. Peter Waldo founded the group in 1170 in Lyons. For his teachings he was excommunicated, but his movement spread. His followers adopted a simple dark habit and sandals. Their teaching was based entirely on the four Gospels. They recognized the scriptures rather than the pope as the final authority and refused to admit to the authority of the Church. Neither did they admit to the Pope possessing "the keys of Heaven."

They developed their own church with its own clergy who took vows of poverty and chastity and rejected three institutions of the Roman Church; purgatory, Mass for the dead and veneration of saints. The sect made considerable headway, especially among the lower classes.

Also, to combat heresy, the Church instituted the Inquisition for detection and suppression. The Inquisition was a gradual growth from the eleventh century on but was well positioned under the direction of the Dominicans by the middle of the thirteenth century. The prime object of the Inquisition was to gain a confession, for only by this could the soul of a heretic be redeemed. When the 'heretic' refused, the confession was extorted, first by friendly persuasion, then curtailment of diet, then prevention of sleep and threat of torture on the rack or strappado.

On the strappado, the martyr was suspended by the wrists, raised to the ceiling, and then dropped to a few inches off the floor-a performance repeated until the sufferer submitted. If no submission, imprisonment and other penalties were meted out. All penalties were expiatory. If later recanted, then the heretic was in expiated and handed over to the State for execution. It should be noted that the numbers of executions, while large, is grossly exaggerated, and it is unlikely that more than ten percent of heretics were convicted. It is generally conceded that the Franciscans and Dominicans did far more to control heresy than either the Crusades or the Inquisition.

By the end of the fourteenth century, the Church was due for a transition. Protestantism was soon to make its advent. We should note here; there are five points that distinguish the Medieval Church from the modem Church.

First, the Medieval Church required compulsory

membership. Secondly, its revenue was derived not only from volunteer contributions but also from fees, tithes and Church property. Thirdly, the Church was a single unified body. Fourthly, the Pope could relax human laws by granting a special dispensation. Lastly, the Medieval Church exercised many functions now provided by the state. By the end of the sixteenth century every one of these principles was to be abandoned.

The Great Reformers

In addition to earlier "Fathers" of the Church such as Augustine, Gregory and others, this study is of fathers emerging out of schisms and founding new sects free from the domination of the Pope. Some of these did more important work than was done by any political group to free men's minds and return a large portion of the Christian world to reliance on the Bible rather than the Church.

Hus

John Hus born about 1369 in Husinetz, Bohemia, and educated at the University of Prague, came early under the influence of John Wycliffe. For his criticisms of the Church, he was excommunicated in 1412. The Pope offered him safe passage to the Council of Constantine to defend his beliefs. In good faith he attended the council, but once he had arrived, the Church ignored the 'safe conduct' promise, tried him for heresy, and burned him at the stake in 1415. Thus. did Hus become one of the earliest Protestant martyrs.

Erasmus

Desiderius Erasmus was born in Rotterdam, Holland in 1465. He became an Augustinian friar. He traveled extensively, visiting many European courts. A scholar rather than a theologian, he attacked the usage of many Latin writers. He wrote a book of maxims from the classics and enlivened them with his own comment. Very early he believed the Bible should be translated into the vernacular. He published an edition of the New Testament in Greek, with a Latin translation and commentary placed in parallel columns with it. He attacked formal religion, claiming that the two great enemies of religion were paganism and outward forms and ceremonies. He saw the need for reform in the Church and thought the time was right for it. However, he wanted gradual reform through education, and always opposed the violence displayed by Luther. He died in Basel, Switzerland in 1536.

Zwingli

Ulrich Zwingli was born in Widhaus, Switzerland in 1484. He was educated at Berne, Basel, and Vienna, and was ordained to the priesthood in 1506. By 1518 he was Pastor in Zurich. His studying caused him to question the authority of the Pope, and he began to attack both religious and social evils, the sale of indulgences and the traffic in mercenary's soldiers. Probably he preached the doctrine of justification by faith before Martin Luther. These two contemporary reformers could not agree on the interpretation of the Eucharist, Zwingly claiming it to be only a symbol, whereas Luther preferred to cling to the older doctrine of transubstantiation. Zwingly fell in battle at Cappel in 1531.

Luther

Martin Luther is probably the best-known name among the religious refo1mers. He was born into a poor family in Eisleben, Ge1many in 1483. Despite his poverty, he was educated at Magdeburg, Eisenach, and the university of Erfurt, where to please his father he studied law. After completion of the law course, he decided to become a monk. And in 1509 he began to teach Aristotle at the University of Wittenberg. He feared that he himself was going to hell, and only after several years of internal struggle did he arrive at the conclusion that one could achieve salvation by faith-a doctrine which he soon began to teach in classrooms.

All is well until 1517 when a transient priest, John Tezel, appeared in Wittenberg and began the sale of indulgences. This sale of indulgences becoming a problem in the Church-there was no repentance for sin required, but for confession and the payment of a certain valuable sum one could obtain a remission of purgatory suffering. Tezel so provoked Luther that he drew up and posted on the door of the Wittenberg Church a series of ninety-five theses attacking and condemning certain evils and abuses in the Church, including the sale of indulgences. These theses were published in Latin and Luther intended that they should be used as a basis for discussion by scholars like himself, but they were translated into German and scattered far and wide throughout the country. During three years, Luther found himself at the crest of a great wave of popularity among the common people, and leader of a great reform movement.

At first the Pope chose to ignore Luther, but his movement seemed to be spreading and so in 1519, Dr. Eck was sent to confute him. In his debate with Eck, Luther stated his beliefs clearly. He said every man should interpret the Bible for himself, and he could approach God without the assistance of a priest as an intermediary; that justification came through faith, not good works, that the early apostles knew nothing of masses, purgatory, pilgrimage, indulgences, or political headship of the Pope. In June of 1520 he was warned to recant and make his peace with the Church, but this he refused to do, and publicly burned the papal bull against himself. This act led to his excommunication in January 1521.

In the summer of the same year he was summoned to the Diet of Worms. Here he was again asked to recant. When he refused, his books were publicly burned, and he was outlawed. The Elector of Saxony, to save his life, kidnaped him and took him into voluntary imprisonment at the Wartburg for a year. While in Wartburg castle, he made the first good translation of the new Testament into German and started a movement to write in German prose.

In 1522 he returned to his teaching in Wittenberg, and he remained there until his death in 1546. For a time, he thought that he could reform the Church from within. Eventually he abandoned that hope and formed the German Evangelical (Lutheran) Church. In 1525 he married a former nun, and his married life revealed his softer and better side. An extremely violent man, he showed many faults and limitations, but tact and tenderness were also on a grand scale.

The common people now had the Bible in their hands and wished to escape the oppression of the Church. The clergy followed Luther readily to escape their monastic vows, and the rulers welcomed the opportunity to seize some Church property. The Diet of Augsburg asked each side to draw up a statement of their fundamental doctrines. The Evangelical Church presented what was to become the "Augsburg Confession" -the doctrine of Luther written up by Melanchthon. This was to be the creed of the Lutheran Evangelical Church.

Lutheranism has always been on the conservative side in reform. It was always oligarchic and governed from above, never democratic like Calvinism. Emphasis was placed on congregational participation in the services, and more freedom of worship allowed than formerly. Today there are perhaps seventy million members of the Lutheran Evangelical Church.

Calvin

John Calvin was born at Noyon, France in 1509. He was educated at the university of Orleans. At first, he started to train for the priesthood, but later changed to law, for which his logical mind admirably suited him. Being influenced by Luther, he avowed Protestantism in 1533 and soon rose to leadership in the movement, becoming one of the signatories of the Augsburg Confession. To escape persecution at home, he moved to Basil and later to Geneva, where he held high civil positions. The close union of church and state under his direction led to a strict moral code enforced by severe civil penalties. But these strict measures led to himself being banished from Geneva for a time. In Church organization he developed a new democratic system of election for all church officers by the congregation, and by having some posts occupied by laymen. The term Presbyterian was applied to the new group, from the Greek word, "presbyter", for pastor or priest or elder.

Calvin gave Protestantism an organized system which

kept it strong through the sixteenth and seventeenth centuries. He was always frank and sincere, able to back up his principles with sound reasoning. His Institutes of Christian Religion is really the first well-ordered treatise on Protestant belief based on the supreme authority of the Bible and the doctrine of justification by faith. His strong conviction of predestination is probably most noted as a Calvinism "trademark." His French translation of the Bible is outstanding and reveals his logical and legally trained mind. He died in 1564, but his movement lived on.

Knox

Calvinism was carried to Scotland by John Knox. Knox was born in 1514 at Haddington, Scotland and was educated at Haddington and the University of Glasgow. After his conversion to Protestantism in 1545, he spent much time on the continent, and there he contacted John Calvin. Calvinism's practical aspects of government and hard work appealed to his Scotch mind, and when he returned home he carried Presbyterianism with him. His Confession of Faith written for Scotch Protestants, is a clear-cut statement of his fundamental teachings. He promoted social welfare and intellectual and religious revival. But was rebuffed by the nobles and died in 1572.

Wesley

John Wesley was one of the latest of the great reformers, not appearing on the scene until the eighteenth century. Born at Epworth, England in 1703, the son of a minister, he was sent to Charterhouse School for Boys, Christ Church, Oxford; and Lincoln College. Not much interested in religion at first, he became an ordained Church of England minister in 1728. In that same year he and his brother,

Charles organized the Holy Club of Methodists at Oxford, so called by their piety and regularity of habits. In 1735 John Wesley came to America, where he was greatly impressed by the simple faith of the Moravians in Georgia.

Returning to England in 1737, he felt himself being "called of God' to preach a new doctrine, and in a few years, Methodism had spread throughout Britain and America. The Methodists made sudden conversion and complete forgiveness of sins the foundation of their teaching. Wesley was a spellbinder preacher with a genius as an organizer. He used the income from the sale of his books to spread the new belief. The press was skillfully exploited with his propaganda. Realizing that social refo1m would give impetus to his movement he provided work for the unemployed, did welfare work among the armed services, and opened dispensaries for the distribution of medicines and the spread of health information. He helped organize the Methodist Episcopal church in America in 1784, and before his death in 1791, the break with the Church of England was almost complete.

At his death, he left a declaration establishing the Methodist Church with one hundred named ministers as a governing body. Vacancies in this body were to be filled by election, and for many years the governing body was filled with ministers only. Today there are two divisions in the conference: the pastoral, made up of ministers, only to discuss and clarify doctrine and policy, and a second body of both ministers and laymen to consider matters of finance. The modem church is a center for social welfare work. It has its own seminaries, colleges, and normal schools for training preachers and teachers. The itineracy of the clergy has been maintained, a minister but rarely holding a post for more than three years.

Individual Reformers
John Wycliffe (1330-1384) Yorkshire, England

John Wycliffe was born about 1320 at Hipwell, Yorkshire. Educated at Oxford, he became master of Balliol College in 1360. A zealous reformer of clergy abuses, he suppolted Parliament in defiance of the Pope, blamed the wealth of the church for many of the evils found therein, proposed that the Bible should be the final authority in matters of religion, and proclaimed that man needed no priest as an intermediate to God.

To facilitate the use of the Bible, he began a translation of it into English in 1378. This translation became the basis of all later English translations and was so well done that Wycliffe has been known since as the father of English prose. Gathering a group of Oxford scholars they became the nucleus of the Lollard movement. Dressed in course red woolen cloth, barefoot and staff in hand, these "poor" preachers moved about peaching this new doctrine to the poor and lowly classes. One finds it not a stretch to liken this approach to those of earlier movements.

They denounced veneration of saints, fasting, indulgences, images-as useless attributes of the Church. They accepted the Augustinian theory of predestination, thus making salvation dependent on Grace rather than merit. The doctrines of confession and transubstantiation were also rejected. More than once John Wycliffe was saved from the canonical authorities by the London mobs. The Lollards were charged with stirring up the discontent that resulted in the Peasant's War. Until he died in 1384 however, the Lollard movement was still on the rise.

1378; Wycliffe began a systematic attack on the beliefs

and practices of the Roman Church. The Lollards, a heretical group, propagated his controversial views.

Sanctuary:
After an accused killer had taken sanctuary in the Westminster Abby, and subsequently arrested, Wycliffe defended the King's servants' (police) lawful right to invade sanctuaries to bring criminals to justice.

1. Theology: Predestination: Strongly supported with this proviso: He believed those in the 'invisible church of the elect' were predestined to be saved rather than the organized and institutional Church members of his day.

2. Transubstantiation: Attacked this dogma because in the annihilation of the substance of the bread and wine, the "cessation of being" was involved. He called it unscriptural and idolatrous, and sought to replace it with the doctrine of remanence (remaining), i.e., the real presence in a non-corporal form. His teachings were challenged by the church, but many formed, in part, the underpinning of the Reformation Movement

3. Biblical authority: He repudiated the authority of the pope and insisted that Christ was the head of the church, and that the Bible instead of church councils and tradition was the supreme authority for Christians.

Wycliffe died in peace in 1384. But his followers were soon facing persecution. Some years after his death, a church council declared Wycliffe's views heretical, ordered his writings burned, and demanded that his remains be removed from consecrated soil. At Papal command his bones were dug up, burned and the ashes cast into a stream.

Susanna Wesley

The following, is from a Wikipedia's article, "Susanna

Wesley" "........although she never preached a sermon or published a book or founded a church, she is known as the Mother of Methodism. Why? Because two of her sons, John Wesley and Charles Wesley, as children consciously or unconsciously will, applied the example and teachings and circumstances of their home life."

1669-1742; she was the 25' of 25 children. Her father, Dr. Samuel Annesley, was a dissenter of the established Church of England. At the age of 13, Susanna stopped attending her father's church and joined the official Church of England. She and Samuel Wesley were married on 11 November 1688. Samuel was 26 and Susanna was 19. Susanna and Samuel Wesley had 19 children. Nine of her children died as infants. Four of the children who died were twins. A maid accidentally smothered one child. At her death, only eight of her children were still alive.

Susanna experienced many hardships throughout her life. Her husband left her and the children for over a year because of a minor dispute. To her absent husband, Susanna wrote: "...because of your long absence, I felt I had to do more than I have yet done. I'd resolved to begin with my own children; in which I observe the following method: I take such a proportion of my time as I can spare every night to discourse with each child apart. On Monday I talk with Molly, on Tuesday with Hetty, Wednesday with Nancy, Thursday with Jacky, Friday with Patty, Saturday with Charles."

Her husband spent time in jail twice due to his poor financial abilities, and the lack of money was a struggle for Susanna. Their house was burned down twice; during one of the fires, her son, John, nearly died and had to be rescued from a second story window. She was the primary source of her children's education.

Her children were not permitted to have any lessons

until they had reached their fifth year, but the day after their fifth birthday their formal education began They attended classes for six hours and on the first day they were supposed to learn the 'whole of the alphabet.' All her children but two managed the feat, and to Susanna these seemed to be very backward. The children got a good education. They all 'learnt' Latin and Greek and were well tutored in the classical studies that were traditional at that time in England.

Not happy with a substitute preacher, Susanna began Sunday afternoon services for their family. They would sing a psalm. Susanna would read either a sermon from her father's or husband's sermon file, and then close with the singing of another psalm. The local people began to ask if they could attend. At one point there were over two hundred people who would attend Susanna's Sunday afternoon service while the Sunday morning service dwindled to nearly nothing. Susanna practiced daily devotions throughout her life. She often shared her experience of the depravity of her human nature and the grace of God. Such was the extraordinary life of *"the Mother of Methodism"*

Chapter 6

Religion in the 19th century

The nineteenth century is a period that is very difficult to evaluate, either from the perspective of religion or from the complexities of church history. Available data is almost overwhelming. At best we can only highlight a few of the major events and trace only a few of the trends.

The century has been called the "age of ideologies." The industrial Revolution had arrived in force; with blessings and bane. New technologies, transportation and communications blessed a few with great wealth, but their "blessings" were many times exacted from the sweat and suffering of the masses.

Political ideologies

Religious and secular reformers were optimists as heirs of the eighteenth-century rationalists. They believed man was inherently good and thus capable of almost unlimited improvement. Many believed that the unequal distribution of property and wealth to be the principle source of evil in society. To improve society all that was needed was a fair distribution of goods. These men were called "socialists."

The most important advocate was Karl Marx (1818-1883), whose book, Das Kapital, proved to be a revolutionary time bomb. He is important to Christianity and religion for his system is militantly atheistic and wherever his teachings have been put in practice the

Church has suffered. One result was that western man came to look for his salvation in political and economic panaceas rather than religion. The teachings of Christ offered great concern for human welfare, but in the eighteenth century the church showed little concern about applying these teachings to the evil of the day.

Organic evolution

When Charles Darwin's book, The Origin of the Species, was published in 1859, probably few people realized the impact it would have on religion. The Darwinian theory, which holds that the higher forms of life descended from the simpler forms, seemed to flatly contradict the Genesis account of a special creation. This hypothesis provided for some that which seemed to be a scientific basis for rejecting special creation and even belief in God. Others found a way of accepting evolution while still holding a belief in God by reducing the Genesis account of creation to a myth. Still others took the view that evolutionary man died off in the great flood, while Noah and family, the "God breathed" man survived, and evolutionary man ceased. This position would answer the question, "Whom did Adam and Eve's children marry?" Pastor Joel Osteen told the story of a young girl who asked her mother, "where did I come from?" The mother told her the best she could that God made her. Then she suggested that she go ask her father. The father told her that she evolved from monkeys. Back to her mother, she said, "you said God made me; daddy said I came from monkeys, which is it?" The mother replied, "He was talking about his side of the family; I was talking about my side of the family."

The idea of the "survival of the fittest" was applied to give a philosophical undergirding to business competition and to rising nationalism. It was believed that through competition for a limited food supply higher forms of life had developed. It was therefore concluded that similar competition would in the business realm produce a superior level for mankind. This kind of thinking led, in the latter decades of the nineteenth century to the most "dog eat dog" competition in economic history. Many applied the same kind of thinking to the various races. The fact that the Germanic and Anglo-Saxon peoples enjoyed economic and military domination over much of the world seemed to indicate that these races were superior on the evolutionary scale.

The acceptance of evolution challenged the Biblical basis of morality. If, after all, man is the product of a long evolutionary process, then any ethical system he might have is also a product of evolution. Since one of man's basic concerns is survival, then any action he takes to protect his survival can be justified (regardless of how immoral these actions may be.)

Biblical Criticism

Christianity, in the nineteenth century Christianity had to fight off wars on many fronts, including having to fight off a violent attack upon the Scriptures from within its own ranks. Those who thus attacked the Scriptures are often called "higher" critics.
Definition:

Lower criticism deals with problems of the texts themselves, trying to prepare the most accurate Bible text possible.

Higher Criticism, on the other hand, deals with such things as authorship and date of Biblical writings. While these are legitimate studies, some of which have been explored here in earlier chapters, the problem arises when men come to the Scriptures with presuppositions that are antagonistic to the idea of divine revelation.

For example: By the end of the century, the generally accepted views of the authorship of the Pentateuch had been questioned, with several authors claiming the first five books of the Old Testament had been written by several authors over a long period of time. Authorship of Isaiah and Daniel were questioned along with refusal to accept Jonah historicity.

The New Testament did not escape these attacks. The historicity of the Gospel accounts was assailed with the claim that were written later and based on earlier documents and sources.

Some held that a conflict existed between the teachings of Christ and the teachings of Paul. Some expressed a preference in the moral teachings of Jesus rather than the theologizing's about Jesus. Later critics demonstrated the difficulty of trying to separate Jesus from the theological teachings about Him

Secularism

A more serious threat to religion and Christianity -Secularism. Secularism; the substitution of worldly values for Christian values so dangerous because it is so all pervasive, penetrating every aspect of the church and because it is so difficult to recognize.

The Industrial Revolution had brought rapid urbanization. Millions of people swarmed to the cities, leaving their religion behind them in far too many cases. Urban life with its sophistication and culture offered many opportunities for further secularization of society. The problem: The Western culture was being dominated by thriving population centers by the end of the century and the church's response was tepid at best with the masses not being reached by the gospel.

The hundred-year period from 1800-1900 saw a great increase in church membership, both in the total number of church members and in the percentage of the population that were church members. Church membership rose from a scant ten percent of the population in 1800 to nearly forty percent in 1900.

Major denominations found growth during this period, yet their relative strength compared to the church at large was lagging. Changes that brought about this diminishing dominance: larger number of immigrants, the birth of new religious bodies, the greater adaptability of some groups to the conditions of the frontier that moved relentlessly westward across the continent.

Social reform movements gave rise to an unprecedented participation of Christians. Christians were active in the anti-slavery crusade, women's rights, prison reform, temperance and peace movements and numerous other refolming ventures. The century was also a time of revivals. From the preaching in the brush arbors of the "Second A wakening" to the great urban revivals of Dwight L. Moody, the nineteenth century witnessed one surge of revivalism after another.

The Slavery Issue

Perhaps there was no greater issue in American history, both political and religious, than the slavery question. Even before the country became an independent nation, anti-slavery sentiment existed.

The most conspicuous feeling was demonstrated by the Quakers, and by 1800 it was spreading nationwide.

During the 1830s the largest discussion was about the colonization plan, which called for the emancipation of the slaves by purchasing the slaves and sending them back to Africa. Because of these efforts, Liberia, in western Africa came into existence.

The plan did not work for there were far too many slaves. About this time the anti-slavery issue took a more radical turn. From the north came the demand that slavery be abolished immediately. The motivation was varied. Some were motivated by politics, some on humanitarian grounds and some by religious beliefs.

Finally, in 1861, words were replaced by swords, and ballots by bullets as the nation blundered its way into the terrible Civil War. But long before this the religious bonds had begun to unravel just as the political bonds would break later. In 1844, the Methodist Episcopal Church had split into Methodist Episcopal North and Methodist Episcopal South. The split came after the Bishop married and slaves came along in the union. Northerners demanded he either get rid of the slaves or set down as Bishop. The southerners insisted he had a right to own slaves. Slavery also separated the Baptists.

Protestantism in Europe

The Industrial Revolution remade Europe politically, socially, and economically. This affected the Protestant movement more than the Catholics in that the Protestants were so involved in some of these trends, such as destructive Biblical criticism, that she could not escape being affected, especially since Protestantism nurtured these trends.

Church of England

While the revivals of the previous century had a beneficial effect on the Church of England, these benefits were now waning. All too often, clerics were perfunctory in performing their duties, services were empty and ritualistic, and members unenthusiastic. But there were exceptions. The Evangelicals kept alive some of the glowing embers of revivalism of the earlier century. Perhaps the greatest contributions of the Evangelicals were the great number of hymns they gave to the church: "Come Ye Thankful People Come," "I Love To Tell The Story," "Take My Life And Let It Be Consecrated, Lord, to Thee" are still widely sung.

The Tractarian movement, or the Oxford movement, sought revival by looking back into the past. It emphasized the value of the ritual and stressed many doctrines such as apostolic succession, that seemed more Roman than Protestant. Some of the leaders became so pro-Catholic in their views that they eventually left the church to join the Roman Catholic Church.

The Nonconformists-the Methodists, Baptists, Congregationalists, Presbyterian and others outside the Church of England, enjoyed a remarkable growth in numbers and prestige during the Nineteenth century. The laws against the Nonconformists were removed, and they enjoyed mostly complete freedom. Perhaps the greatest preacher in nineteenth century England was Charles H. Spurgeon, a Nonconformist. Through the lives of committed individuals, Christianity made itself felt in Great Britain. William Wilberforce headed a movement that eventually abolished slavery in the British Empire. Many government officials were motivated to make their religion meaningful in public office. William Gladstone, prime minister four times, was perhaps the outstanding example of a Christian in politics.

Protestantism on the Continent

In Germany the church was greatly affected by the unification of the numerous German states into one Germany in 1870. This led in some respects to less control over the affairs of the church. German scholars, such as Schleiermacher, Kant, and Ritsclh were leaders in the negative criticism and speculative theology preciously mentioned. Yet most Germans remained staunchly loyal to their church and were more likely to be influenced by Pietism than by the attack of the scholars.

Liberalism became strong in the state church in the Netherlands leading to more than one secession during the nineteenth century. In the Scandinavian countries, Protestantism, predominately Lutheran, enjoyed a revival. Pietism was on the upsurge and missions were advanced. Danish Lutheranism produced Soren Kierkegaard, practically unrecognized in his own time, but now regarded as one of the century's outstanding theologians.

Italy and Germany

The Protestant organizations in Italy faced continual oppression from the Roman Catholic Church. Highly placed Protestant clergy called upon the Roman Church to give the same freedom of religious convictions to minorities in Italy that they themselves expect to get in countries where they are in the minority. The deportation of Rex Paden in 1955, after eight years as organizer of the evangelistic Church of Christ, is indicative of the enmity between the Roman Catholic hierarchy and the burgeoning Protestant movement.

Germany

The official National Socialist (Nazi) Party program stated that it stood for a positive Christianity without binding itself to any confession. From the first it took a stand against the organized churches, both Catholic and protestant. Probably the official view best stated was in the "Myth of the Twentieth Century" by Rosenberg, which was required reading for all the Nazi party and is the one of the few on the Roman Catholic "Index" today. Rosenberg outlined a "religion of blood' or race, setting forth a belief in the supremacy of the German man. To fit the mold, Christianity had to be purged of every trace of Judaism. The Old Testament was to be abolished and replaced by a collection of Nordic sagas. The 'superstitious" parts of the New testament were to be rejected, and the teaching about human brotherhood and humility were to be revised. The crucifix was discarded, together with a belief in Christ as the "lamb" of God. A new register of martyrs and "saints of the blood" was composed of Germany' s World War I heroes.

The creed of Nazi Germany ran as follows: "I believe in the God of German religion, who fights for the nobility of man; and in the struggle of my people. I believe in the helper-in-need, Christ, who fights for the nobility of man, and in Germany where the new humanity is being created." Baldur von Schirach proceeded to instill the idea of a state religion in the two Nazi youth movements, the Hitler Youth, and the Federation of German Girls. He exhorted them: "Stand together. Fight for Adolf Hitler. Fight for our German Fatherland. If you do this, you are fulfilling THE WILL OF GOD.

Religion is used countless times to justify immoral behavior. It's not difficult to conclude that the Nazi religion was linked to their obsession with the supremacy of the German bloodline and the vilification of the world's minorities. Their hatred for the Jews and Judaism was culminated in the death camps where their "German religion" was ghastly displayed. The Birmingham massacre of 2016 is another example of "religious" fervor that views superiority of one race over another to the end that the despised must be eliminated and the "pure" stock remain untainted.

Chapter 7

Religion in the nineteenth century continued
Revivalism

Again, divisions occurred in some of the frontier religious bodies. The "excitements" wore thin but the churches in general had lasting results. The frontier played an important part in reshaping the altering the relative strength of the major denominations. On the frontier the Methodists and Baptists fared better than the older, more respected churches, such as the Congregationalists, Presbyterians and Episcopalians. In fact, by 1850 the Methodists and Baptists became the two largest groups in the land.

As revivalism and church planting growth accelerated, camp meetings became less important. But other revival forms took their place. Men like Lyman Beecher, who ably defended the orthodox position against growing Unitarianism in New England; Charles G. Finney, revolted against radical Calvinism, a communion in which he had been raised; preached a message of "free and full salvation." Finney enjoyed outstanding success in Eastern cities, and later became President of Oberlin College in Ohio, which became the center of revivalism and anti-slavery sentiment.

In 1857 a financial panic struck several northern cities. The panic was unusual in that it was largely responsible for bringing "laymen" into leadership of revivalism in these cities. It began in New York City when a janitor left the door ajar in a downtown church, open for noonday prayer services. The prayer meetings grew until they became common in other cities. The Young Men's

Christian Association, which had just begun, played a significant role in the revival. The most well know evangelist of the century, Dwight L. Moody, came from the "laymen." He had been a successful shoe salesman and turned to religious service. For the next forty years, Moody's voice was heard across the land and even across the sea in Britain where he held several successful campaigns. Teamed with Ira Sankey, a gifted song leader, Moody was by far the most widely known and successful mass evangelists of the century.

The latter three decades of the Nineteenth century brought a growing pluralistic society. Immigration increased significantly during this period, to such that the historic position of numerical superiority enjoyed by the Anglo-Saxon, Protestant culture was threatened. The immigrants came from Eastern and Southern Europe. The result was a substantial increase in membership in Roman Catholic and Orthodox Churches and in Jewish congregations.

Urbanization:

The patterns of evangelism and nurture seemed adequate for rural society but failed to reach the millions who flocked to the cities. One effort to meet this challenge was the "Institutional" church which sponsored educational and social activities along with their traditional services. A church famous for this new approach was Philadelphia's Baptist Temple, ministered to by Russell H. Cromwell. Eventually the effort resulted in the founding of Temple University. In 1880, the Salvation Army, founded in England, made its way to America, where it rendered an invaluable service to the cities' down and outers.

The Social Gospel;

The social gospel movement came out of ethical and social challenges. The Industrial Revolution and its growth came with attending evils; Individual pietism that worked well in rural America, could not cope with the changes. Business ethics of this period were disturbing, yet the private lives of these new 'barons' were mostly without reproach with many becoming outstanding church leaders.

New frontier religious bodies: Three groups:

The United Brethren in Christ, came into being in 1800. Philip William Otterbein, a German Reformed minister and a close friend of Francis Asbury, along with Martin Boelm, a Mennonite, were the leaders of this new group, with a doctrine like the Methodists. This group united to form the United Brethren Church.

Evangelical Association:

A German group in its origin, was founded by Jacob Albright. The denomination also closely resembled the Methodists in doctrine and policy. In 1934, the two groups merged to form the Evangelical United Brethren Church.

The Christian Church
(Disciples of Christ), Church of Christ and the Christian Church

Out of the "Great Second Awakening" in early 19th century and in the midst of the disunity and escalating negative 'party spirit' among Christian denominations, there came a Scottish theologian to the emerging American frontier with a message; the principles by which a reformation of the church according to the authority of the New Testament could be attained. Thomas Campbell's 'Declaration and Address" is probably the most significant documents the Restoration Movement has produced.

Thomas Campbell, father of Alexander Campbell, both of Scotland and both Presbyterians, were all to familiar with schisms and church splits. They were of the Old Light Anti-Burgher Seceders branch; one of the twenty-one Presbyterian factions at the time. Not only was Campbell influenced by his Presbyterian background, but he was also influenced by the writings of John Locke. In Locke's A Letter Concerning Toleration, a parallel to the Declaration and Address' major themes, especially that of Toleration, one can recognize the like-mindedness.

In Locke's Letter on Toleration: "However clearly, we may think this or the other doctrine to be deduced from scripture, we ought not therefore to impose it upon others as a necessary article of faith because we believe it to be agreeable to the rule of faith."

Campbell's Declaration: "Although inferences and deductions from Scripture premises, when fairly interpreted, may be truly called the doctrine of 'God's holy word', yet are they not formally binding upon the consciences of Christians farther than they perceive the connection and evidently see that they are so."

In his scholarly history of the movement, "The Disciples of Christ" (1907) author Errett Gates noted that while Thomas Campbell focused on the need for Christian unity, Alexander emphasized the need for the authoritative pattern of the New Testament church. In so doing, Gates argues that Alexander shifted the chief point of the movement away from union. Gates was seen by many as a liberal, educated at the University of Chicago Divinity School, and one who wanted to downplay any concern for

Biblical authority on the part of the early leaders. However, conservative Homer Hailey had picked up the same theme. Quoting Gates at this very point, Hailey contends that by 1813, the Campbells had "begun to shift the emphasis from the obligation of Christian union to the authority of primitive Christianity." This seems to endorse the attitude of many conservatives that the main thrust of the Restoration Movement is to emphasize the pattern of New Testament Christianity. Many of these conservatives have no interest at all in unity.

It is important to note that which Thomas Campbell says in his Propositions within the Declaration and Address. More of his Propositions deal with New Testament authority than church unity. However, Campbell was just as concerned with New Testament authority as much as he was with the need for Christian union. To picture him in any other posture is to misunderstand him.

For the 50 years following the famous Kentucky "Cane Ridge" arbor revival, this movement grew faster than any other group; and today remains the largest indigenous religious body in the United States

Later Movements

The Quakers

The society of friends, or Quakers, was founded by George Fox in 1647. It aimed at the restoration of a primitive Christian religion. They were distinguished by simplicity of dress and life. All ceremonial, including even the lord's supper, was abolished. They denounced war. George fox was born in England in 1624.

In his 20s, fox claimed to receive a revelation, and began

to call men to a life exemplary of the indwelling light and power of Christ. He opposed both the High-Church professors who clung to ancient tradition and the purists who clung to scripture. He removed the emphasis from the expiatory death of Christ to the living Christ in the human heart. Among his ten talents (a list of 10 beliefs) the following represent his unorthodoxy:

1. Spiritual baptism and spiritual communion only-no sacraments whatsoever.

2. The spiritual equality of the sexes (new for his day)

3. In the assembly, no one was to speak until moved by "the spirit" to do so.

4. The priesthood of all believers (new for his day)

Quakerism was transplanted to the new world by William Penn., and the Quakers settled in what was to become known as the "Quaker state," Pennsylvania. From early colonial times, the term 'quaker or quake' has been synonymous with honesty and square dealing.

The Deists

Deism had its main growth after the reformation. It is a natural system of religion, based on science and logic, and apposed both to atheism, which denies the existence of god, and to any religious system based on a belief in a god who reveals himself to man. It is thus antagonistic to Christianity, Mohammedanism, Buddhism and pantheism. Since deism is based on indisputable fact, it is capable of expansion and elevation with every increase in knowledge of the universe. Only part of the Christian new testament is accepted, the rest is opposed claiming it is irrational, clearly false, and morally objectionable. Hell is a loving god impossibility.

Deism is not simply an intellectual conception, but it is a practical religion. Because of its basis in reason, it has broad appeal to the modem intellectual. The say all religion is based on the golden rule Note: it is commonly accepted that the great majority of early "founding fathers" of this nation were Christians, therefore we are a Christian nation. However, a closer study indicates, although no belief system dominated the group, deism was the religion of many signers of the constitution.

The Mormons

The church of Jesus Christ of latter-day saints is usually called "Mormon" because of the divine authenticity of the book of Mormon. Their belief system basically stated: since god is invariable and no respecter of persons, his laws are immutable, and that whatsoever he gives by revelation is a law to the Saints. Their Thirteen Articles of Faith outlines their doctrine.

The following are a few of those Articles that differ with mainline Christian theology and religion. "...all mankind can be saved through the atonement of Christ by obedience to the laws and ordinances of the Gospels."

"We believe the Bible to be the Word of God insofar as it is correctly translated. We also believe the Book of Mormon to be the Word of God."

"...We believe in the gifts of tongues, of interpretation of tongues, of prophesy, of visions, of revelation, of healing by faith."

"...God will yet reveal many great and important things concerning the Kingdom of God."

"...That Zion will be literally built on this continent and Christ will personally reign on this earth, that the earth will be renewed and receive its paradisiac glory."

The Mormon Church has three standard works besides the Bible that it views as authoritative and inspired scripture. These are the Book of Mormon, Doctrines and Covenants, and The Pearl of Great Price, the first being the most widely known outside the church.

Joseph Smith, the founder, was born of farming people in Sharon, Vermont, December 23,1805. At early age he believed himself to receive messengers from heaven. Of these the angel, Moroni was chief, and he revealed to the boy the knowledge of the existence and whereabouts of the Book of Mormon. Additional dreams: The Book of Mormon was entrusted to his care with a key to its translation. Moroni revealed that he had buried the sacred record on the year 420 in the hill Cumorah in Northern New York State. The Urim and Thummin which Joseph Smith was to use as keys were described as two transparent stones set in the rim of a bow attached to a breastplate.

From these "plates" Joseph Smith translated the unsealed portion and in 1820 was published as The Book of Mormon. Smith and his followers maintain that in 1820 Smith was ordained by John the Baptist and made an Apostle. On 1830, the Church of Christ of Latter Day Saints was established at Fayette, New York, with Smith its first prophet.

Mormon prophets and apostles teach that God the Father was once a mortal man who continually progressed to become a God (an exalted being) and that the rest of mankind can become gods like him by adopting and faithfully adhering to Mormonism.

As Mormon general authority Milton R Hunter put it, "today then, God the eternal Father, our Father in Heaven, is an exalted, perfected, and glorified Personage having a tangible body of flesh and bones."

A temple, built in Kirkland, Ohio; Missouri became a center. They met with disfavor and persecution in many quarters largely because plurality of wives was permitted. Smith was assassinated in a Carthage jail, June 27, 1844, and the presidency descended to Brigham Young. After a large portion of the Nauvoo settlement, the largest Mormon group in Missouri, was attached and annihilated, continued persecution drove them farther and farther westward. In the fifteen-hundred-mile trek to the basin of the Great Salt Lake the Mormons lost another thousand of their followers. Here they dwelt in a time of peace and established the great temple in Salt Lake City. In 1850 the Territory of Utah was organized as part of the United States of America.

In 1952 there were over one million followers, dispersed in three districts, or Stakes of Zion, extending from southern Alberta to the northern boundary of Mexico. Today there are over 16M followers worldwide with 30,000 congregations, 67,000 missionaries and 188 published languages.

A chief concern has been their attitude toward women. But since monogamy has been enforced this criticism has been lessened.

RUSSELLISM (Jehovah Witnesses)

Russellism is a mixture of Universalism, Unitarianism, Adventism and Materialism. This conglomeration of religious vagaries was originated by Charles T. Russell, commonly called "Pastor Russell."

C. T. Russell was born on February 16, 1852 at Pittsburgh, Pennsylvania. He founded Zion's Watch Tower (1879) which today is known as The Watch Tower Announcing the Jehovah's Kingdom.

The Finished Mystery, his seventh volume, caused a split in the organization with the larger group following J. F. Rutherford and under whose leadership, "The Society" became known by its present name "Jehovah's Witnesses."

Russell first published his tenets under the name, "Millennial Dawn," but later brought them out under the title of "Studies in The Scriptures." His writings were mostly un-scriptural and anti-scriptural, although there was just enough truth to make them plausible enough to be doubly deceiving. He enriched himself greatly from the sale of his books.

Mr. Russell's character as a man was nothing of which to boast. A court in Pennsylvania ruled that he tried to perpetuate a fraud upon his wife and denied his plea of being penniless when his wife sued him for divorce. It was later developed that he had transferred $317,000 to the Watch-Tower Bible and Track Society, of which he was president, seemingly with the intent to avoid paying his wife alimony. His wife obtained her divorce from him because of his unmanly conduct and gross familiarity with other women. Open court testimony concerning his character recorded his saying of himself, "I am like a jelly fish; I float around here and there; I touch this one and that one, and if she responds, I take her to me, and if not, I float to others." Russellism teaches:

The following points are from the six volumes of Scripture Studies and the Watch-Tower God:

There is only one person in the God-head. Christ:

That Christ was a "created angel" before he came to this earth. That Christ was not a combination of "two natures-human and divine."

That Christ did not atone for the sins of the race.

That Christ's body was not raised from the dead.

111

That Christ is forever dead That Jesus was not divine until after the resurrection.

That Christ was no longer the same person after the resurrection.

That Christ is not a mediator.

The Holy Spirit:

That the Holy Spirit is only the influence or power exercised by the one God.

That the Holy spirit is not a personality.

The Kingdom:

That the Kingdom is not yet established That the kingdom is not to be established until the Millennium.

Note: Quoting from THE WATCHTOWER, no. 4, 2017, location of Paradise, "Clearly the concept of a lost Paradise is a golden thread running through human history." While Witnesses claim Jesus and the Apostles have been living on earth since 1874, and His Earthly Kingdom was established in 1914, yet this watchtower article reports, "Those then living will enjoy a 'Paradise' as well as God's favor, both of which Adam lost. .... The hope of Paradise on earth is one that God promised long ago. What a wonderful prospect the Bible offers-paradise (on earth) forever." No mention of a "millennium" in this article.

Heaven:

Reject the orthodox belief in a heaven with Christ for believers, but only a restored earthly paradise in which, "that Kingdom is a world government in the hands of Jesus Christ that will replace all human rule."

Sin:

That each does not die for his own sin, but for Adam's sin.

Conversion:

That God is not trying to convert sinners in the Gospel-age, but that conversion begins in the Millennium.

A Second chance:

That every man shall have another chance.

Death:

That death is a destruction; that death is annihilation; that death is unconsciousness.

But the regenerated person will live again on earth forever

Hell:

That there is no eternal punishment.

The Lord's Supper:

That the Lord's Supper took the place of the Passover feast. That the Lord's Supper should be observed annually.

Baptism:

That baptism is added to the scheme of redemption That water baptism symbolizes the baptism of the heart.

Time Setting:

That the apostles and Christ have been living on the earth since 1874 as invisible spirits in bodily form.

That all worldly kingdoms will end in 1914 and the Church of Christ will be set up with Christ as Head.

That the harvest of the Gospel age was to end in 1914.

Russell continued his teaching until his death in1916 aboard a transcontinental train in Texas.

Seventh-day Adventists

Adventism began in Massachusetts in 1831, under the leadership of William Miller. In 1833, in Low Hampton, New York, he began to preach that the end of the world was at hand, publishing a pamphlet entitled, "Evidences from scripture and history of the second coming of Christ about the year 1843, and of His Personal Reign of One Thousand Years."

When this prophesy failed, he declared that he had erred in his calculation and set the time in 1844. This also failed, and he set the new date of 1845. The third failure divided his followers and out of the fragments Seventh-day Adventism was constructed. Adding some new doctrine, the principle one of which was Sabbath keeping, that is Saturday; to this time all the followers of Miller had kept Sunday. Elder James White and his wife, Ellen, became the leaders of the Seventh-day branch of Adventism.

Because of various divisions, there are now six bodies of Adventists, viz: Advent Christians, Church of God, Churches of God in Jesus Christ, Evangelical Adventist, Life and Advent Union and Seventh-Day Adventist. As a rule, all these divisions now wait for the second coming of Christ without making any attempt to set the date thereof. Three things characterize all Adventist teaching: Prophesy, the Sabbath and the sleep of the soul.

Seventh-Day Adventist teaches:

1. There are two separate laws given at Sinai; one written in stone and the other written by pen and related only to ceremonial laws.

2. That the ceremonial law ONLY was nailed to the cross and that the Decalogue is still binding.

3. That we are to keep the Sabbath Day.

4. That the decalogue was not done away in the abolition of the Old Covenant.

5. That the soul sleeps after death

6. That it doesn't make any difference what name you wear.

114

7. That the observance of the Lord's Supper at regular intervals is unimportant

8. That we may expect Christ's return any time now.

Baptism: Jewish and Christian

Although the term "baptism is not used to describe Jewish rituals, the purification rites in Jewish laws and tradition, called "Tvilah", have some similarity to baptism, and the two have been linked. The "Tvilah" is the act of immersion in natural sourced water, called a "Mikva". In the Jewish bible and other Jewish texts, immersion in water for ritual purification was established for restoration to a condition of "ritual purity" in specific circumstances. For example, Jews who (according to the Law of Moses) became ritually defiled by contact with a corpse had to use the mikvah before being allowed to participate in the Holy Temple. Immersion is presently required for converts to Judaism as part of their conversion. Immersion in the mikvah represents a change in status regarding purification, restoration, and qualification for full religious participation in the life of the community, ensuring that the cleansed person will not impose uncleanness on property or its owners. It did not become customary, however, to immerse converts to Judaism until after the Babylonian captivity. This change of status by the mikvah could be obtained repeatedly, while Christian baptism, is, in the general view of Christians, unique and not repeatable. Even the so-called rebaptism by some denominations is not seen by them as a repetition of an earlier valid baptism and is viewed by them as not of itself repeatable.

Baptism and Early Christianity

John the Baptist adopted baptism as the central sacrament in the messianic movement, seen as the forerunner of Christianity. Baptism had been part of Christianity from the start, as shown by the many mentions in the Acts of the Apostles and the Pauline epistles. Christians consider Jesus to have instituted the sacrament of baptism. How explicit Jesus' intentions were and, in the view of many, whether he envisioned a continuing organized Church and is a matter of dispute among scholars.

There is scholarly consensus that the earliest Christian baptism was normally by immersion, or at least that this is possible. The church most likely practiced full immersion, partial immersion and affusion at various times and places in the early centuries, with sprinkling being practiced rarely (and probably only for medical reasons). By the third and fourth centuries, baptism involved catechetical instruction as well as chrismation, exorcism, laying on of hands and recitation of a creed. Affusion became the normal mode of baptism between the twelfth and fourteenth centuries, though immersion was still practiced in the sixteenth century. In the sixteenth century, Martin Luther retained baptism as a sacrament, but Swiss reformer Huldrych Zwingly considered baptism and the Lord's supper to be symbolic. Anabaptists denied the validity of infant baptism, which was the normal practice when their movement started and practiced believer's baptism instead. Several other groups, notably the Baptists and Dunkards, and later by the Christian Churches have always practiced baptism by immersion as following the Biblical example. Current 'Faith' and 'Bible' churches also practice baptism by immersion.

Baptism modes have been a source of controversy beginning in early Christian history. Equally controversial; the saving quality of Christian baptism, with its opposing factions dividing faith groups for centuries. Note: See the "Faith Only" article in this study for further insights into this important issue.

Chapter 8

Modern Eastern Religions

This study could include an account of the many Eastern nations and their multiple religions, which study can be found elsewhere. However, considering current political unrest, a brief study of Korea, China and Japan and their religious history should be helpful.

North and South Korea

Main religions: Cheodoism or (Chondoism) is a religion with deep roots in Confucianised indigenous shamanism. It is the religious dimension of the Donghak ("Eastern Learning") movement that was founded by Choe Je-u (1824-1864), a member of an impoverished yangban (aristocratic) family. In 1860, in reaction to the rise of "foreign religions" which in his view included Buddhism and Christianity, he founded Chondoism after having been allegedly healed from illness by an experience of Sangje or Haneullim, the god of the universal heaven in traditional shamanism. The Donghak movement became so influential among common people that in1864 the Joseon government sentenced Choe Je-u to death. Yet 30 years later, the movement had grown in that the members gave rise to the "Peasant Revolution" against the royal government. With the division of Korea in 1945, most of the Chondoist community remained in the north, where most of them dwelled.

Chondoism is the sole religion flavored by the North Korean government and is regarded by the government as its "national religion" in that they identify it as a "revolutionary anti-imperialist" movement.

Korean Shamanism (Muism)

Religion of the shin(hanja:-gods) is the ethnic religion of Korea and the Koreans. In contemporary Korean language the shaman-priests or Mu is known as a mudang if female or baksu if male. Korean mu "shaman" is synonymous with Chinese wu, which defines priests both male and female. The role of the mudang is to act as intermediary between the spirits or gods, and the human plain, through gut (rituals), seeking to resolve problems of development of human life.

Central to the faith is the belief in Hwanin, meaning the "source of being", and of all Gods of nature, the utmost god or the supreme mind. The mu are mystically described as descendants of the "Heavenly King", son of the "Holy Mother (of the Heavenly King")", with investiture often passed down through female princely lineage. However, other myths link the heritage to the traditional.

Numbers:*
Non-religious, 64.3%
Shamanism, 16%
Chondoism, 13 .5%
Buddhism, 4.5%
Christianity, 1.7%, and growing with 500 home churches (many 'underground')
(10,000 Protestants, 1000 Catholic reported)
* World Christian Encyclopedia, 2015

North Korea's Kim Jong Un is a despotic leader. While

imprisoning many Christian missionaries and Pastors, he takes affront to their calling the people to worship God and demands that all worship him as God. This God neuroses is not unique to Kim, but other historical despots have demonstrated the same neurosis, such as Adolf Hitler who claimed, "worship me as God;" then later said, "worship Germany."

A short list follows of men who destroyed thousands of their cult lives by naming themselves either God or Jesus Christ: Arnold Potter, 1804, Adventist; trying to prove that he was God's Son, he died in an attempt to "ascend into heaven" by jumping off a cliff. His body was later retrieved by his followers and burned.

John Thom, !799, Cormish tax rebel, claimed to be "Savior of the World."

William Davies, 1833, said his second son was to be "God the Father."

Marshall Applegate, 1931, "I'm Jesus, Son of God." All his followers committed mass suicide.

Sun Myung Moon, 1920, He claimed that he and his wife were the "True Parents" of mankind and the restored Adam and Eve."

David Koresh, 1959, "the Son of God, the Lamb." Mass suicide.

Jim Jones 1931, "reincarnation of Jesus." Followers committed mass suicide.

Buddhism and Confucianism

Buddhism entered Korea from China in the 4th century. Confucianism entered also from China a short time later. Buddhists makeup a small minority in North Korea today. In South Korea they are the majority with 43% of the population. South Korea's ancient religions are still active along with all the world's major religions, peacefully coexisting with shamanism. Some traditions are best understood as important cultural properties rather than rites of worship. Shamanism in the daily life of the common man is connecting with the spiritual world and making predictions about the future.

Current South Korean major religious bodies. Protestant: 34% with 8 million faith to Dangum, male son of the Heavenly king and initiator of the Korean nation.

Korean Muism has similarities with Chinese Wuism, Japanese Shinto, and with the Siberian, Mongolian, and Manchurian religious traditions. The mudang is similar to the Japanese Miko and the Ryukyuan Yuta. Muism has exerted influence on some Korean new religions, such as Chondoism in North Korea. Many Christian churches in Korea make use of practices rooted in Shamanism as the Korean shamanic theology has affinity to that of Christianity. In the late 1890s Protestant missionaries gained significant influence while earring out campaigns of physical suppression of local cults. There is no knowledge about the survival of Korean shamanism in contemporary North Korea. Many northern shamans, displaced by war and politics, migrated to South Korea. Shamans in North Korea were and are of the same type of those of northern and central areas of South Korea.

North Korea

In the light of recent North Korean aggressive behavior, i.e., nuclear warfare, and their recent persecution of religious groups, especially American Christians, relevance drives further information concerning the status of religion in North Korea.

In the United States, many North Korean Chaldean

Christians have sought asylum claiming religious persecution in North Korea. Recently two dozen of these 'refugees' were refused entry in that they had already gained legal status in Germany. The U.S. government claimed that there was no continuing hardship. These Koreans were in El Cajon California where presently 60,000 Chaldean Christian immigrates live.

The Term Chaldean relates to a 1552 A.D. break by ethnic Assyrian Christians from the Assyrian Church of the East to the Roman Catholic Church, and since that time this body has been known as Chaldean Christians. The word, Chaldean, comes from an early Hellenistic designation of an area of South Eastern Babylonia, called Chaldea. These with their early presence along with strong Christian missionary efforts have greatly influenced social, political and religious life in the Koreas for five centuries. However, since the communists party has controlled North Korea, religion including Christianity has suffered heavy persecution, causing a heavy shrinkage in the number of religions adherents. But recent reports are encouraging;

Roman Catholic: 20% with 5 million
Buddhism: 43% with 11 million
Muslim: less than 2% with 40,000 plus another hundred thousand foreign workers from Muslim countries, particularly Indonesians, Malaysians, and Pakistanis.

South Korea

South Korea has one unique distinction. In the heart of Seoul, is home to the world's largest congregation, the Full Gospel Central Church, formerly known as The Yoido Full Gospel Central Church. Its founder, Mr. David Yonggi

Cho has retired as head Pastor several times, but the church has run into immediate infighting among the remaining ministers, causing him to come out of retirement, most recently late in 2006. Membership reached 10,000 in 1970. Having outgrown its original location, the church searched for a new place to build. Yoi Island, in the middle of the Han River was chosen as the new location, with its first service in 1973. Within a month the church hosted the 10th Pentecostal World Conference with 55,000 attending including 5,000 foreigners.

Connected to the World Assembly of God Fellowship; (Pastor Cho was elected chairman in 1992) the congregation is also a leader in the Full Gospel Businessmen's Fellowship International. Beginning in the 1990s, the church decided to establish satellite churches throughout the city of Seoul and further afield, as it could not keep expanding indefinitely. Despite the drain of members to the satellite churches, new recruits by the mother church-brought through the vast cell network-have made up for the losses. As of 2007, membership stood at 830,000, with seven Sunday services translated into 16 languages. The church is served by 171 associate pastors and 356 lay pastors.

The church has established many ministries as part of its outreach program. A representative sample follows:

Prayer Mountain; tiny cubicles in which people may lock themselves to fast and pray.

Church Growth International; dedicated to teaching church growth principle to Pastors all over the world.

World Evangelical Center; a ten-story educational institution attached to the church.

A television studio; built to broadcast worship services worldwide. The Full Gospel Educational Research Institute; to promote evangelism and theological training

The Elim Welfare Town; a facility for the elderly, the young, the homeless and the unemployed

In 1986, the church established Hansei University.

Using the Seoul church satellite model, hundreds of western churches have seen their churches' attendance dramatically increase within a few years. One congregation in Oklahoma City, reaches 75,000 in Sunday attendance with 13 satellite campuses and 36 ministries.

Present Chinese religions

During the Cultural Revolution in the 1960s and 1970s, all religions were repressed. Churches, temples and mosques were destroyed, and many people were killed and tortured to drive people from religion. Later however, in the countryside in some eastern and northern provinces, Chinese Christianity stilted to grow very quickly as the Chinese went from village to village peaching. Consequently, in some villages and small country towns, most of the people professed Christianity. The repression fueled the growth, though it was not unusual to have Christian leaders imprisoned.

The growth came from conversion. Unlike other Chinese religious adherents, Christians in China became Christians by change of faith and not by birth. In China people who are born into Muslim families are considered Muslim if they simply don't eat pork or follow other "Muslim" customs. People are considered Buddhist or Taoist if they simply pay homage at ancestral tombs and believe that their ancestors are with them spiritually. But becoming a Christian in a hostile society is a matter of faith and is voluntary.

Chinese Christians must believe that a man born thousands of years ago and thousands of kilometers away to an unknown alien people was the Son of God. The death, burial, resurrection of a man who died in a foreign count1y means forgiveness of sins and salvation. One must believe this man created the universe. These beliefs are strange and outside traditional ways of thinking about the nature of human life and the cosmos.

Christianity in China has survived in a hostile environment. In the past hundred years, Christianity has taken root. Tens of millions have become baptized Christians. Once known as the religion of the peasants, after 1989, it started to spread among the educated people and business people in coastal cities like Shanghai and the economic zones. It is reported that Christians now number more than 5% of China's population or about 75 million.

Chinese Christianity is different than Europe or American Christianity in that women are usually the leaders in the churches and house church groups. Chinese Christianity tends to be Pentecostal. That means that they regularly pray for miracles and believe in miraculous "gifts of the spirit."

Japanese Religions

Shinto, is the indigenous religion of Japan, practiced by nearly 80% of the population with 100,000 shrines and 79,000 priests. It is defined as an action-centered religion, focused on ritual practices. Early writings do not indicate a unified "Shinto religion", but rather to a collection of native beliefs and mythology. Shinto today is a term that applies to the religion for public shrines devoted to a multitude of gods (kami) The word, Shinto, is made up of two words; "shin" meaning spirit and "to" meaning philosophical path or study.

After World War II, Shinto sects and new religions, with

new found freedom, articulated in Japan's constitution providing space for proliferation of new religious movements. Scholars in Japan have estimated that between 10% and 20% of the population belongs to the new religions with a Buddhism sect the largest with about 10 million members.

Buddhism: Arrived in Japan in the 6th century from Korea. Buddhism was functional to affirm the state's power and mold its position in the broader culture of East Asia. Japanese aristocrats set about building Buddhist temples in the capital of Nara, and then in the later capital of Heian (now Kyoto). Now the most popular branch is "Pure Land Buddhism". It emphasizes the role of Amitabha Buddha and promises that reciting the phrase "Nama Amida Busta" upon death will result in being removed by Amitabha to the "Western Paradise or the "Pure Land", and then to Nirvana. Another prevalent form of Buddhism is Nichiren Buddhism, which was established in the 13th century. A controversial denomination, whose political wing forms the komeito, Japan's third largest political party. Common to most linages of this denomination is the chanting. As of 2007, there were 315,000 Buddhist monks, priests and leaders in Japan. By 2014 that number increased by 60,000.

Christianity

Christianity was introduced into Japan by Jesuit missions in 1549. The missionaries were successful in converting large number of peasants, former Buddhist monks, and members of the warrior class. By 1569 there were 30,000 Christians and 40 churches. In the 1560s the number rapidly to 100,000. In the domain of Christian local lords, non-Christians were forced to accept baptism and shrines.

Buddhist temples were converted into churches or destroyed.

For the next four centuries Christianity went from an accepted religion to one that was many times outlawed. Yet each time persecution came, the Christians continued to worship in secret. Today there are 1-3 million Christians in Japan most of them living in the western part of the country where missionary activities were centered in the 16th century. In 2007 there were 32,000 Christian priests and Pastors in Japan. Among many Japanese some Western customs originally related to Christianity (including Western style weddings, Valentine's Day and Christmas) have become popular as secular· customs among many Japanese.

Islam

Islam in Japan is mostly represented by small immigrant communities from other parts of Asia. In 2008 it was estimated that 80-90% of the Muslims in Japan were foreign born migrants primarily from Indonesia, Pakistan, Bangladesh and Iran. It has been estimated that the Muslim immigrant population amounts to 70,000-100,000 people, while the "estimated number of Japanese Muslims ranges from thousands to tens of thousands."

Demographics; Japanese Buddhism, 34%,
Shinto Sects, 3%
Christianity, 1 %
Non-religious (folk Shinto), 52%

Protestantism in Germany and Italy

The Protestant organizations in Italy faced continual

oppression from the Roman Catholic Church. Highly placed Protestant clergy called upon the Roman Church to give the same freedom of religious convictions to minorities in Italy that they themselves expect to get in countries where they are in the minority. The deportation of Rex Paden in 1955, after eight years as organizer of the evangelistic Church of Christ, is indicative of the enmity between the Roman Catholic hierarchy and the burgeoning Protestant movement.

Germany

The official National Socialist (Nazi) Party program stated that it stood for a positive Christianity without binding itself to any confession. From the first it took a stand against the organized churches, both Catholic and protestant. Probably the official view best stated was in the "Myth of the Twentieth Century" by Rosenberg, which was required reading for all in the Nazi party and is the one of the few on the Roman Catholic "Index" today. Rosenberg outlined a "religion of blood' or race, setting forth a belief in the supremacy of the German man. To fit the mold, Christianity had to be purged of every trace of Judaism. The Old Testament was to be abolished and replaced by a collection of Nordic sagas. The 'superstitious" parts of the New testament were to be rejected, and the teaching about human brotherhood and humility were to be revised. The crucifix was discarded, together with a belief in Christ as the "lamb" of God. A new register of mru1yrs and "saints of the blood" was composed of Germany's World War I heroes.

The creed of Nazi Germany ran as follows: "I believe in the God of German religion, who fights for the nobility of man; and in the struggle of my people. I believe in the helper-in-need, Christ, who fights for the nobility of man, and in Germany where the new humanity is being created." Baldur von Schirach proceeded to instill the idea of a state religion in the two Nazi youth movements, the Hitler Youth, and the Federation of German Girls. He exhorted them: "Stand together. Fight for Adolf Hitler. Fight for our German Fatherland. If you do this, you are fulfilling THE WILL OF GOD.

Religion is used countless times to justify immoral behavior. It's not difficult to conclude that the Nazi religion was linked to their obsession with the supremacy of the German bloodline and the vilification of the world's minorities. Their hatred for the Jews and Judaism was culminated in the death camps where their "German religion" was ghastly displayed. The Birmingham massacre of 2016 is another example of "religious" fervor that views superiority of one race over another to the end that the despised must be eliminated and the "pure" stock remain untainted.

Germany's Cold Religion
from: Christianity Today

Berlin based journalist, Markus Spieker, says the Protestant state church is dead. "The percent of committed Christians is maybe 3-4%. Eighty percent belong to a church nominally, Protestant or Catholic. A mere 0.5 percent belong a free evangelical church. The percent of people who believe in life after death is less than 50 percent. It's what a German philosopher, Ruediger Sanfranski, calls "cold religion," very left brain, very cognitive, focused on rituals and membership but not on personal commitment. Sometimes the mainline bishops say we need to be more mission minded. But they don't put any money into it.

There are those who ask, is there something about German culture that keeps the church from growing? Their generational families, going back to Luther, were strong enough to launch a would changing culture of Christianity and at times paid the price for that call to religious freedom. Yet over the last century and a quarter, the German culture; religiously, militarily and philosophically pointed away from "God dependency" to State dependency with Church complicity.

U.S.S.R

Marx' often quoted, "religion is the opiate of the people," along with his opposition to religion in that it supported the idea of private property, was adopted by Lenin, and we find the latter requiring that all Communist leaders renounce religion. Following the Revolution, all churches were closed, and the chapels destroyed. Most of the property of the Russian Orthodox Church was confiscated, including six hundred of the thousand monasteries and convents, the sacred vessels and vestments, all the real estate, and the hoard of Church treasure estimated at one and a half billion dollars. The priests were deprived of all control over education, marriage, divorce, registrations births and deaths. Resistance led to arrest, and some of those arrested were executed by firing squad. Religious services were discouraged but allowed under permit. The press opened a campaign against it, with two magazines motivated by this object. Education was directed toward the same end. A "Society of the Militant Godless" was organized.

Under Joseph Stalin, with pressure on many founts, came a change of policy. People were permitted to hold any religious belief, but religious services were confined to purely religious pursuits with no charitable or educational work allowed. The censes of 1937 showed that still one-third of the urban and two-thirds of the rural population in the Soviet Union was Christian.

The Beginning of the Twentieth Century
The Armenian Genocide

The first half of the century exposed he most heinous of human expressions. The first 'expression' was the genocide of two million Armenians living in Turkey. Religion again was at the root of this tragedy. Turkey was Moslem, Armenia was Christian.

The Turks were mostly the 'common' people, herdsmen, farmers, hill people, with limited education. The Armenians were the minority upper class with higher education and culture, holding many of the high governmental offices. The capital of Armenia was Ani, called the "city of a thousand and one churches."

The Ottoman Empire began crumbling. Three young Turks led a 1913 coup with the intention of building a new Turkish Empire. The problem: Armenia stood between Turkey and their empire goal of reaching to the middle of Asia. The first World War was engaged in western Europe. The Turks believed that the world would have its attention on that area, and that the "Armenian question" could be settled without undue attention. Result: Two million Armenians were killed, and their old civilization practically erased as their institutions, art, edifices, and culture were targeted for destruction.

The decision to annihilate the entire population came directly from the ruling triumvirate of the ultra-nationalistic Young Turks. The actual extermination orders were transmitted in coded telegrams to all providential governors throughout Turkey. Armed roundups began on the evening of April 24, 1915, as 300 Armenian political leaders, educators, writers, clergy and dignitaries in Constantinople were taken from their homes, briefly jailed and tortured, then hanged or shot. The Armenian men were next. They were dragged from their homes, tied together in small groups, taken to the outskirts of their town and shot dead or bayoneted by death squads.

Then followed the women, children, and the elderly. They were ordered to pack a few belongings and be ready to leave on short notice under the pretext that they were being relocated for their own protection. They were taken on death marches heading south toward the Syrian desert. Their possessions were taken, and their houses quickly occupied by Muslim Turks. The children, in some cases, were spared from deportation by local Turks who took them from their families.

The children were coerced into denouncing Christianity and becoming Muslims and were given Muslim names. For Armenian boys the forced conversion meant that each had to endure painful circumcision as required by Islamic custom.

The caravans consisting of thousands of deported Armenians were escorted by Turkish governments. These guards, for 'fees' allowed both Turkish government units of hardened criminals to attack defenseless people, killing as they pleased. They also encouraged Kurdish bandits to raid and steel anything they wanted. In addition, an extraordinary amount of sexual abuse and rape of girls and young women occurred at the hands of these bandits. Many of the most attractive women were kidnaped for a life of involuntary servitude. The death marches involving over a million Armenians covering hundreds of miles and lasting months. Indirect routes were chosen to keep the caravans away from Turkish villages.

An estimate; 75% of the Armenians perished, especially children and the elderly. Those who survived were herded into the desert with nothing to eat and no water. Others were killed by being thrown off cliffs, burned alive, or drowned in rivers.

Pleas to the western powers met with sympathy, but no real help. Not until the Russians moved west, militarily, into Turkey did the Armenians get relief. However, in 1917, the Russian troops withdrew upon the Russian Revolution. About 500,000 Armenians survived by going with the Russians and occupying small regions which were once part of their homeland. There the Armenian leadership declared the establishment of the Republic of Armenia. The "Young Turks" fled into Ge1many and into asylum. Germany refused to return them. Later Armenian activists found their hiding places and assassinated them along with two of their followers.

Woodrow Wilson, engineered a treaty that was signed in 1920, establishing the Republic of Armenia. Turkish nationalism soon reared its ugly head again as new revolutionaries deposed the moderate leadership and refused to honor the 1920 Treaty of Survest. Turkey expelled any surviving Armenians, including thousands of orphans. Only a tiny remnant would then live in the easternmost area of the former part of historic Armenia and as part of the Soviet Union.

Current data on religious groups are as follows: The predominate religion; Christianity. The official name of the Armenian church; Armenian Apostolic Church; founded in AD 40-60 by two of the twelve apostles,

Thaddaeus and Bartholomew

Over 93% of Armenian Christians belong to the Armenian Apostolic Church, a very ritualistic, conservative church. The Armenian Evangelical Church has a vely strong presence with several thousand members, its roots going back to 1846. Catholics also exist in Armenia; both Latin rite and Armenian rite Catholics. Armenia is home to the Molokans, which practice a form of Spiritual Christianity; originated from the Russian Orthodox Church. The Jewish community diminished to 750 persons since independence with most emigrants leaving for Israel.

Religion and World War II

Rather than write about the events and results of World War II, of which most are aware, we shall deal here with only the religious aspect.

A conservative public intellectual, George Weigel writes, "the collapse in the restraining power of religion helped to push the world into the era of total war." Russian writer, Alexander Solzhenitzen had once asked, why, in 1941, a Europe "bursting with health and abundance" had "fallen into a rage of self-mutilation"; and he offered the same explanation for all the disasters of the early 20th century; man had "forgotten God."

In Western Europe, Protestant and Catholic clergy struggled to explain the seemingly senseless horrors of the war to their flock. Mr. Weigel lists the secular ideas that were supplanting religion before 1914. They include: racial theories based on the superiority of the Slavic or Teutonic peoples, and their incomparability with each other; Friedrich Nietzsche's glorification of destruction and power; distorted forms of Darwinism which saw the survival of the fittest as a prescription for an endless arms race. He thinks that religion itself was corrupted by secular nationalism, to the point where many of Europe's clergy saw nothing but merit in killing fellow Christians of a different nation. He concluded; *"Religion can either restrain the urge to fight or exacerbate it. Sometimes both factors are at work simultaneously. Religion can mitigate conflict within a large group but also increase the chances of conflict between those large groups. A century on from the Great War religion seems in many places to have retained its power to exacerbate strife but lost its capacity to calm and restrain."*

Chapter 9

Into the Twenty-First Century

During the last 120 years, there have been significant theological changes, possibly more than for any like period in history. In earlier generations changes in doctrine came about very slowly, with generations, even centuries passing before any important changes being evident. In early pre-Christian history, most belief groups were so geographically separated from each other, that change agents were of little effect outside their local homeland. Changes came with wider social, cultural and religious exposure.

Theological changes most evident:

Theological Liberalism, sometimes known as protestant liberalism, is a theological movement rooted in the early nineteenth century German Enlightenment, notably in the philosophy of Immanuel Kant and the religious views of Frederick Schleiermacher. It is an attempt to incorporate modern thinking and developments, especially in the sciences, into the Christian faith. Liberalism tends to emphasize ethics over doctrine and experience over Scripture authority. While essentially a 19th century movement, this liberalism came to dominate 20th and into the 21st centuries. Liberal Christian scholars embraced and encouraged the higher biblical criticism of modem Biblical scholarship.

Protestant liberal thought in its most traditional incarnations emphasized the universal Fatherhood of God, the brotherhood of man, the infinite value of the human soul, the example of Jesus, and the establishment of the moral, ethical Kingdom of God on earth. It has often been relativistic, pluralistic and non-doctrinal. Liberalism birthed other movements with varying emphases. Among these movements have been the Social Gospel, Theological Feminism, Liberating Theology, Process Theology, and the Jesus Seminar. One product of these movements is the Myth of Christian Origins which denies the divinity/deity of Christ and the authority of scripture.

Advocates of the Social Gospel rendered an important service in calling attention to the many social ills affecting modem society, but as time passed, the easy optimism of Liberals was no match for the demonic forces being unleashed all over the world. Of more lasting impact has been modem Liberalism's impact upon American denominations. Liberals infiltrated denominational structures and soon controlled them. Educational boards, benevolent enterprises, publishing houses, mission boards and colleges were before long in the hands of men of liberal persuasion. From the beginning, liberals were in leadership positions in the Federal Council of Churches of Christ in America, which began to operate in 1908, and later in the World Council of Churches.

Strong opposition began to surface from conservatives. Struggles developed in several major denominations, leading to bitterness and even division. Among those groups refusing to go along and splits occurring, were the Baptist churches, Christian Churches, and a sizable minority of Congregation churches, refusing to become a part of the United Church of Christ.

The conservative cause was strengthened by new conservative publishing houses with reputable authors defending the fundamentals of the gospel; an infallible Bible, the deity, the virgin birth, the bodily resurrection of

Christ, the substitutionary atonement, and the second coming of Christ. These advocates became known as "fundamentalists." Unfortunately, this term began to carry overtones of reproach that suggested that fundamentalists were obscurantist, opposed to all progress.

Challenges: The Twentieth Century into the Twenty-First Century

Just as Christianity had its challenges in the nineteenth century, the twentieth/twenty-first centuries brought a new wave of challenges and their responses.

1. Secularism

Especially in the West, Secularism has posed the most persistent challenge to all faith groups especially to Christianity. Since the Renaissance, man has increasingly looked to himself as the source of values. In the process he has pushed God into the background. Secularists are not going to put faith groups under persecution, in that the trademark of these modems is "tolerance," a bland indifference that puts a premium on a stance of non-commitment. In this age Secularists assume Christianity is irrelevant. Men no longer need to look to God for help, for science can provide all he needs. Young people often find life work and calling in science, rather than a call to Christian service. Why? In this country there is a great push to study science in the public schools, while the study and even any practice of religion has all but been pushed out by public apathy and a series of Supreme Court decisions.

In this writer's high school days, there were weekly 'home-room' Bible/devotions and in most cases led by a Minister or other community religious workers. Faith groups dominated many of the 'after hours" activities. There were no 'non-religious' schools. However, segregation was a fact of life. There were separate schools for Catholics and Blacks. Only a hand full of Jewish families lived in and around the city, so their children were part of the 'white' schools. When it came to integration a few years later, it was "social conscience" not the church (religion), that led the way. The question again is asked, "does religion move culture or does culture move religion?"

2. Communism

This nineteenth-century ideology of Karl Marx became a threat when communism swept to power in the Bolshevik Revolution in Russia in 1917. Communism, avowedly atheistic and anti-religious, is dramatically summarized in a simple statement of Marx, "religion is the opiate of the masses," and used by the ruling classes to control the working classes. When they came to power, the communists began indoctrinating their people in atheism, trying their best to eliminate the church, which in this case was the Russian Orthodox Church. Churches and seminaries were closed, priests were executed, or exiled and religious festivals were abolished. In part, the violent action against the church stemmed from the fact that the church in Czarist Russia often worked hand in hand with the Czars' oppressive policies.

Amazingly the campaign failed to stamp out religion in Russia. Today the Orthodox Church claims as many as fifty million members and there are as many as six million members of Baptists or Evangelical churches scattered across Russia. Wherever Communism has gone the story is somewhat the same: In central and eastern Europe, the church, whether Protestant, Roman Catholic, or Orthodox, has been persecuted with stifling restrictions. In China the church has suffered even more severely. As soon as the communists took over, all foreign missionaries were executed, imprisoned or exiled. The Chinese Christians, once numbering three million adherents, suffered untold hardships and for a long period the church was facing entire eradication. Later in this study, statistics will show a revival of Christianity in China unequaled in any other country with exciting new numbers.

3. Nationalism

The threat is especially noted among new nations that have recently gained their independence. These African and Asian nations have been the recipients of 150 years of western missionary efforts. Yet in many of these nations, doors have now been closed to missionaries. In both official actions and in raising local native hostility to anything resembling Western imperialism, nationalism has in many clear cases created antagonism toward Christianity while reviving non-Christian religions such as Buddhism, Hinduism and Mohammedanism.

4. Theological liberalism

As the twentieth century emerged the religion of modem man was facing escalating challenges. Liberalism was the new and most threatening challenge even though sheltered at first behind many higher education doors. This "new" theology rejected the doctrine of human depravity (one of Calvinism's basic beliefs), and took a rather light view of sin, so their belief in the ultimate perfectibility of the human race could come to pass. Social and personal evils were not, as they believed, the result of sin but of ignorance. Education, they believed, would alleviate most if these evils.

Theological Liberalism, sometimes known as protestant liberalism, is a theological movement rooted in the early nineteenth century German Enlightenment, notably in the philosophy of Immanuel Kant and the religious views of Frederick Schleiermacher. It is an attempt to incorporate modem thinking and developments, especially in the sciences, into the Christian faith. Liberalism tends to emphasize ethics over doctrine and experience over Scripture authority. While essentially a 19th century movement, this liberalism came to dominate 20th and into the 21st centuries. Liberal Christian scholars embraced and encouraged the higher biblical criticism of modem Biblical scholarship.

Protestant liberal thought, in its most traditional incarnations, emphasized the universal Fatherhood of God, the brotherhood of man, the infinite value of the human soul, the example of Jesus, and the establishment of the moral, ethical Kingdom of God on earth. It has often been relativistic, pluralistic and non-doctrinal. Liberalism birthed other movements with varying emphases. Among these movements have been the Social Gospel, Theological Feminism, Liberating Theology, Process Theology, and the Jesus Seminar. One product of these movements is the Myth of Christian Origins which denies the divinity/deity of Christ and the authority of scripture.

Advocates of the Social Gospel rendered an important service in calling attention to the many social ills affecting modem society, but as time passed, the easy optimism of Liberals was no match for the demonic forces being unleashed all over the world. Of more lasting impact has been modem Liberalism's impact upon American denominations. Liberals infiltrated denominational structures and soon controlled them. Educational boards, benevolent enterprises, publishing houses, mission boards and colleges were before long in the hands of men of liberal persuasion. From the beginning, liberals were in leadership positions in the Federal Council of Churches of Christ in America, which began to operate in 1908, and later in the World Council of Churches.

Strong opposition began to surface from conservatives. Struggles developed in several major denominations, leading to bitterness and even division. Among those groups refusing to go along and splits occurring, were the Baptist churches, Christian Churches, and a sizable minority of Congregation churches, refusing to become a part of the United Church of Christ.

The conservative cause was strengthened by new conservative publishing houses, with reputable authors defending the fundamentals of the gospel; an infallible Bible, the deity, the virgin birth, the bodily resurrection of Christ, the substitutionary atonement, and the second coming of Christ. These advocates became known as "fundamentalists." Unfo1tunately this term began to carry ove1tones of reproach that suggested that fundamentalists were obscurantists, opposed to all progress.

Social reform would occupy most of the liberals' energy. The "Social Gospel" was different than earlier social reform movements that had limited goals; the abolition of slavery, the abolition of liquor, etc. However, this group wanted to reform the whole structure of society. Since the reforms, they thought, could not be changed by pure piety, they resorted more and more to legislative means to reach their goals.

Neo-Orthodoxy

Neo-orthodoxy in Europe, also known as theology of crises and dialectical theology, was a reaction against doctrines of 19th century theology and a reevaluation of the teachings of the reformation. Karl Barth is the leading figure associated with the movement. Following are the basic theological points of this theology:

Revelation

Neo-orthodoxy strongly emphasizes the revelation of God by God as the source of Christian Doctrine. In contrast Natural theology, whose proponents include Thomas Acquines, states that knowledge of God can be gained by a combination of observation of nature and human reason. This issue remains a controversial topic within some circles to this day.

Transcendence of God

Most neo-orthodox thinkers stressed the transcendence of God. Barth believed the emphasis on the immanence of God had led human beings to imagine god to amount to nothing more than humanity writ large. He stressed the "infinite qualitative distinction" between the human and the divine, a reversion to older Protestant teachings on the nature of God. Paul Tillich attempted a medium course between strict transcendence and ontological analysis of the human condition.

Existentialism;

"......the analysis of individual existence in an unfathomable universe and the plight of the individual who must assume responsibilities for acts of free will without any ce11ain knowledge of what's right or wrong or good or bad," Mirriam-Webster. Reinhold Niebuhr, Karl Ba.1th, and earlier, Soren Kierkegaard, were critics of the then fashionable liberal Christian modernist effort to "rationalize" Christianity-to make palatable to the "cultured despisers of religion." Kierkegaard maintained that Christianity is "absurd" (i.e., it transcends human understanding) and presents the individual with paradoxical choices. The decision to become a Christian, Kierkegaard thought, is not fundamentally rational but passional-a leap of faith. Neo-orthodoxy opponents reply that without a foundation or support (such as from science) for faith it is simply fabrications of fallen human imagination, and in effect constitutes idiolatry. They have applied the term, fideism, (a blatant refusal to find support for the faith outside one's own circles) Some of these opponents have gone so far as to claim greater affinity with atheism in that regard than with the "theological and cultural trappings of so called Christendom" Diedrich Bonhoeffer's "religion-less Christianity" venomously denounced this stance as well as did Kierkegaard's later works.

Sin and Human Nature

In Neo-orthodoxy, sin is seen not as mere error or ignorance; it is not something that can be overcome by reason or social institutions. It can only be overcome by the grace of God through Jesus Christ. Sin is seen as something bad within human nature itself. This amounts to a renovation of historical teachings about original sin. This core conviction about the universality and intransigence of sin has elements of determination and has not surprisingly offended those who think people are capable, wholly or in part, of effecting their own salvation (i.e., synergism). In other words, neo-orthodoxy might be said to have a greater appreciation of tragedy in human experience than either conservatism or liberalism.

Influence upon American Protestantism

From its inception, neo-orthodoxy has largely been unacceptable to Protestant evangelicalism. Why? Because neo-orthodoxy generally accepts biblical criticism; has remained mostly silent on the perceived conflicts caused by evolutionary science; and, in espousing these two viewpoints, it retains at least some aspects of 19th century liberal theology. This is in keeping with its stated aim not to commit to specific theories of verbal inspiration of the Bible, seeing them as utterly subordinate to Jesus' transformative life, death and resurrection.

The Ecumenical Movement

Recurring international tragedies, and the shadow of nuclear destruction have caused many theological differences, once important enough to divide brothers, to pale into insignificance. The strength of Christianity's foes has caused many to cry, "Unite or perish!" Beyond these reasons, is a growing conviction that God desires a united church, that division is a sin. In other words, men have become convinced that the "church is essentially, intentionally, and constitutionally one" and are now seeking means to implement this unity.

Issues between Roman Catholic-Eastern Orthodox

The mutual anathemas (excommunications) of 1054, marking the Great Schism between Western (Catholic) and eastern (O1thodox) branches of Christianity, a process spinning several centuries, were revoked in 1965 by the Pope and the Ecumenical Patriarch of Constantinople. The Roman church does not regard orthodox Christians as excommunicated, since they personally have no responsibility for the separation of their churches. In fact, Catholic rules admit the Orthodox to communion and the other sacraments in situations where the individuals are in danger of death or no O1thodox churches exist to meet the needs of their faithful. However, Orthodox churches still generally regard Roman Catholics as excluded from the sacraments and some may even not regard Western Catholic sacraments such as baptism and ordination as valid.

In 2006, Pope Benedict XVI and Patriarch Bartholomew I of Constantinople met for the first of two meeting out of which came The Declaration of Ravenna, a significant rapprochement between the two positions. The declaration recognized the Bishop of Rome as the Protos, or first among equals of the Patriarchs. The acceptance and the entire agreement was hotly contested by the Russian Orthodox Church, the acceptance of which highlighted the existing tensions between the Patriarch of Constantinople and the Moscow Patriarchate

A major obstacle to improved relations between the Orthodox and Roman Catholic Churches has been the insertion of the Latin term flioque into the Niceno-Constantinople Creed in the 8th and 11th centuries. This obstacle has now been effectively resolved. The Roman Church now, obliging the Eastern Church's "who proceeds from the Father," profession of the creed, adds, "and the Son," (both referencing the Holy Spirit as proceeding from the Father)

The Eastern tradition giving expression firstly to the Father's character as first origin of the Spirit, and the Western expression, "and the Son (flioque)" giving expression firstly to the consubstantial communion between Father and Son; and it believes that provided this legitimate complementarity between Father and Son and does not become rigid. It does not affect the identity of faith in the reality of the same mystery confessed.

Continuing dialogue at both national and international levels continues between the Roman Catholic and Orthodox Churches.

Issues within Protestantism

Contemporary developments in mainline Protestant churches have dealt a serious blow to ecumenism. The decision by the U. S. Episcopal Church to ordain Gene Robinson, an openly gay, non-celebrate priest who advocates same-sex blessings, as bishop, has led the Russian Orthodox Church to suspend its cooperation with the Episcopal Church. Likewise, when the Church of Sweden decided to bless same sex marriages, the Russian Patriarchate severed all relations with the church, noting that "Approving the shameful practice of same-sex marriage is a serious blow to the entire system of European spiritual and moral values influenced by Christianity."

Bishop Hilarion Alfeyev commented that the inter-Christian community is "bursting at the seams". He sees the great dividing line -or "abyss" not so much between old churches and church families as between "traditionalists" and "liberals", the latter now dominating Protestantism. He predicted that other northern protestant Churches will follow suit, and this means that the "ecumenical ship' will sink, for with the liberalism that is materializing in European Protestant Churches, there is no longer anything to talk about.

However, there are several new organizations dedicated to encouraging ecumenical cooperation among Protestants, Eastern Orthodox, and, at times, Roman Catholics. Some European and American universities are now offering degrees in "Ecumenical Studies" in which theologians of various denominations teach their respective traditions, and at the same time, seek common ground between these traditions. In addition, an increasing trend has been that of the sharing of church buildings by two or more denominations, either holding separate services or a single service with elements of all traditions.

One drawback to uniting with other believers is that attitude mostly demonstrated by conservatives that, "I'm right and others are wrong". What feeds this attitude? A pride of ignorance, which to overcome may require a grasp beyond Unity's reach. Having no religious interplay with others outside one's own faith system results in an ignorance of other faith traditions, and many times even a hostility toward others with that which seems to be a contrarian or even heretical 'religion'. For these, both individuals and groups, unity with "liberals" is tantamount to total surrender to the forces of darkness.

The World Council of Churches

Another movement, to address church unity, felt the need for a more comprehensive organization to encompass larger areas of cooperation. Plans for such an organization were laid, but these had to wait for the end of World War II before they were consummated. The World Council of Churches came into being at Amsterdam in 1948 and numbered more than one hundred religious bodies. The number included major Protestant bodies of Europe and North America, several of the Orthodox churches, and most of the "younger churches" of Asia and Africa. The most recent meeting was held in New Delhi where the Russian Orthodox Church was admitted. By this meeting more than two hundred bodies had joined. A separate group, The World Council merged with the Federated Council, into what is known now as the National Council of Churches; an American council. Conservatives felt they could not be a part of the liberal atmosphere of this council created the National Association of Evangelicals, without any interest in promoting mergers.

The approach of Roman Catholicism to Christian Unity: Since Roman Catholics believe that theirs is the only true church, the solution is relatively simple-erring non-Catholics can enjoy unity any time they want by returning to the Roman Church. However there have been indications that some church leaders have taken a more conciliatory attitude toward some effort to unite. The last generation of Popes have shown merger sympathy as well. Many feel that the World Council has a concern for organization and bureaucracy that precludes the possibility of real unity based on solid Biblical faith. Critics of the World Council also see in it the danger of a super church that might be a threat to Christian liberty.

Responses:

Many see these challenges as God's chastening hand, used to revive His people. A look at some of the signs that the church, even though purged, show the church's resilience with powers to meet these new challenges. In the last 70 years, the United States has experienced a revival rather than a spiritual depression. The crusade efforts by Billy Graham stand out as the early principle producer and he as the leader of this revival. Even if this revivalist model has somewhat run its course, there are other efforts that represent 'new' models of missionary work. One example of new world-wide mission/evangelizing work is that of Franklin Graham, Billy Graham's son, with his worldwide

"Samaritan Purse."

Another sign of growth in missionary endeavors, from 1960 with 42,000 Protestant foreign missionaries at work, to that number presently almost doubling. Encouraging also is that of a growing maturity in local churches on the foreign fields. Many missionaries have stressed an "indigenous" church model whereby local leaders are developed to carry on the work once foreign support is withdrawn. Further growth indicators; renewed interest in Biblical scholarship and theology, studies with historical and cultural implications, new Bible translations, the founding of hundreds of Bible Colleges and Institutes many in response to Protestant Liberalism. A growing number of these institutions have converted with full regional accreditation to traditional university models. "Servant Leaders" is a growing designation of these Christian college and university students as they enter a sectarian world with its need for a Jesus 'servant-hood" ministry regardless of the students' occupational or professional pursuits. This contrasts with earlier years where conservative Christian higher education opted for a "full time ministries" recruiting and curriculum model.

Within the 'new university' model, there are 'colleges' providing multiple educational disciplines i.e., example; Pacific Christian College, with its surviving name, mission and heritage is now one of the five colleges of Hope International University (Calif). Each of the five offers both undergraduate and post graduate degrees. Contrary to some of the college's supporters' concern that its mission and enrollment would be compromised in such a merger, the opposite has been true with enrollment more than doubling over the last few years.

Traditionally, major denominational colleges and universities have structured their ministerial curriculum with a twostep system. The first step being a four-year undergraduate Liberal Arts program. The second, a three-year Seminary study relating basically to theology, religion history, and ministerial functions. Conservative institutions as described above, while adopting this traditional model, are giving acknowledgment to the cultural, sociological and religious challenges of the 21st century as they strive to adapt their mission to these challenges without surrendering their core beliefs.

Chapter 10

Challenges in the 21st Century
Witchcraft

Belief in witchcraft has existed throughout recorded history. This belief has appeared in many and diverse ways among cultures and religions worldwide, both primitive and "highly advanced "cultures. In the Western world, historically, witchcraft derives from Old Testament laws against witchcraft. Yet it entered the mainstream when belief in witchcraft gained some church approval in the Early Modem period. It posits a theosophical conflict between good and evil, where witchcraft was generally evil and often associated with the Devil and Devil worship. From intense opposition from Christian fundamentalists to intense belief, and in some churches even approval, the 'old witchcraft' has been renamed to 'contemporary witchcraft' and has been so named in a branch of modem paganism. It is no longer practiced in secrecy.

There is a new, yet old, story, USA Today, recently reported that in Uganda witch craft is alive and 'prosperous'. The story: A mother found the dismembered body of her ten-year-old daughter in a pit under an outhouse. The girl had gone to fetch water in a nearby swamp when she was abducted, strangled and dismembered. Body parts were found miles away. The mother was quoted, "I was shocked when I saw the mutilated body of my daughter, I really couldn't believe if she was really my daughter. She was missing almost every part of her body. She died a very painful death." police later arrested a wealthy neighbor, businessman, who authorities alleged used Jane as a human sacrifice in a witchcraft ritual designed to bring him good fortune. "He confessed to me that he carried out the ritual to boost his dwindling business," The man is now in prison awaiting trial. "He said he knew the act would bring him good luck and success in life."

Her experience is only too common in Uganda, where multiple sacrifices occur every year despite the government's efforts to stop it. Kyampisi Childcare Ministries, which rehabilitates children lucky enough to escape the ritual, report that thousands of children go missing in Uganda annually and dozens are likely victims of sacrifice.

Fueling the practice are witch doctors and believers willing to kill and offer body parts to dark spirits to get rich, heal diseases, mitigate misfortune, forestall impending events or even help their favorite candidates with elections. A Ugandan police commissioner commented, "Sometimes spirits may demand a certain body part of the child. If you can be able to get it, then this becomes currency to exchange with the evil spirits so that they grant you success. Each body part has ace1tain retail value. Private parts demand the highest fee.

Prosperity Gospel and 'seed faith'

Such questionable and similar belief and practices, as noted in witchcraft, have been chronicled in every modem nation for decades (even centuries) only under sanitized applications with different religious terminology. The term witchcraft is seldom used, but a somewhat parallel practice is applied. Hence: for an offering to the enabler, one who has a 'direct line to God' promises the following should, will, must, possibly happen to bring good fortune, success in life, but the 'Biggy' is, disease healed.

Religious systems like Abundant or Prosperity Theology and "seed faith" theology when applied in Pentecostal practices has led in many cases to unfortunate ends. "Seed faith' is based on the proper idea that giving is better than getting. As the Catholic Church discovered to its shame in the late Middle Ages, people eager to make a buck can easily twist this truth. If you work for charity, there is a fine line between urging people to give to good works and urging them to give to you.

A quick check reveals that one famous preacher /evangelist/faith healer, recently appeared again on American TV after worldwide healing crusades, has a net worth of $40 million.

The Mary Cult

In 1981, six children claimed to experience visions of the Virgin Mary. It launched a following that continues today and has led some of the faithful to extremes. Terry Colafrancesco founded the self-contained religious Cult, that was in 2017, a center piece of an hour-long TV network program depicting it is as strikingly similar to other radicalizing cults. For example; they photographed teens 'escaping' in the middle of the night, being picked up by family members in the woods beyond the compound, a scene reminiscent of TV coverage of similar episodes inside and outside the Scientology Cult compounds in Los Angeles and Hemet, California.

The Mary Cult's home base in called Caritas of Birmingham. This community is the home of many Mary devotees, but has also been the center of controversy. Another TV program, (a Marian Apparition commercial), cited five 'Facts' known about the following,

1. Miracles do happen (Marian Apparitions)
2. Sightings of Mary
3. The Vatican has approved only 16 Apparitions
4. First known MA; 1914
5. More visions in Caritas than anywhere else. To date, the Vatican has not acknowledged the Caritas Apparitions.

The Cult draws 'pilgrims' from around the world who seek miracles; especially physical healing. The obvious financial gains have filled the groups treasury with Colafrancesco the sole official.

Women far outnumber men who come to the compound. Some have suggested that the veneration of Mary gives women representation in and about God's throne, a maternal relationship to the Godhead, or, the Trinity.

Citing from the Official Catechism of the Roman Catholic Church, published in 1995 (the first official Catechism in 400 years); Pages 273.276, Part One, begins, "The Most Blessed Virgin Mary", "there in the glory of the Most Holy and undivided Trinity"…"in the communion of all the saints, the church is awaited by the one she venerates as Mother of her Lord and as her own Mother." "The Most Blessed Virgin Mother when her earthly life was completed was taken up body and soul into the glory of heaven, where she already shares in the glory of her Son's Resurrection, anticipating the resurrection of all members of the body. We believe that the Mother of God, the new Eve, the Mother of the Church, continues in heaven to exercise her MATERNAL role in behalf of the Church."… "from the most ancient times, the Blessed Virgin has been honored with the title, 'Mother of God,' to whose protection the faithful fly in all their dangers and needs ... This special devotion differs essentially from the adoration which is given to the incarnate Word and equally to the Father and to the Holy Spirit, and greatly fosters this adoration." .... "The liturgical feasts dedicated to the Mother of God and Marian prayer, such as the Rosary, an "epitome of the whole gospel and express the devotion to the Virgin Mary."

Cults: History, Definition, Groups and Doctrine

The First Amendment, ratified in 1791, affirmed that "Congress shall make no law respecting an establishment of religion or prohibiting the free exercise thereof."

James Madison wrote, "The religion...of every man must be left to the conviction and conscience of every man...We maintain, therefore, that in matters of religion no man's right is (to be) abridged by institution of civil society."

As was stated in an earlier chapter, while every man is free to choose whatever expression of religion belief, not every religion is equally true or healthy or equally beneficial to every person. Nor is it saying that every religion yields equal eternal results. In light the First Amendment, and quoting Ron Rhodes, (The Challenge of the Cults) "it is safe to say there will never be a Theological Federal Communications Commission, or a Spiritual Pure food and Drug Administration. Today this freedom has produced a vast melting pot of religious ideas, including cultic ideas, with many Americans drinking richly from this pot."

Today there are over twenty-five million Americans involved in the cults and occult. This makes it very clear that cults have taken advantage of religious freedom to spread their unorthodox and sometimes dangerous doctrines.

Why this radical change in America's Religious landscape? Again, Rhodes shares these observations:

×   Rapidly eroding spiritual foundations:

×   Most people holding to moral relativism.

×   A Christianity that is only one choice in a vast smorgasbord of religious options.

×   Impotent and lifeless churches, biblical immaturity, spiritual dryness among members, thus making them open to seeking out options.

×   A deluge of cultic and occult groups vying for the American mainstream.

×   An incredible increase in Eastern religions

×   A cultic and occult penetration of American businesses, health facilities, and public schools via the New Age movement.

×   A pervasive disillusionment and lack of direction among America's youth making them vulnerable to cultic leaders who promise black and white answers to today's toughest dilemmas.

×   A shifted family structure, with many children growing up in single-parent households-many of which provide little or no religious foundation for the children.

This is the age of 'tolerance." One risks being accused of intolerance if he/she should say anything negative about another's religious beliefs. Yet to "tolerate" something that can severely damage another person whether in this life or in eternity, to many, would be evil. Cult damage has long been reported in the media with the following examples: Jehovah's Witnesses who have tragically and meaninglessly died as a result of refusing blood transfusions; the little children who died painful deaths for the reason that medical treatment was avoided because the parents were Christian Scientists who believe sin, sickness, and death are mere illusions; and the little children who have been sexually abused within "The Children of God" (now known as "The Family"), a cult known for "flirty fishing" (luring people into their prostitution circles). Who can forget the hundreds of people who died in the Jonestown tragedy. Dr. Paul Martin, former Director of the Wellspring Retreat and Resource Center (that provides counseling and help for ex-cultists members) reports that 185,000 Americans alone join a destructive cult each year. Of those at least 25% will suffer enduring irreversible harm that will affect their ability to function adequately in the social, emotional, family and occupational domains.

Definition: Cults

There are those who say one should not use the word, "cult" with its negative connotations. Instead they prefer terms like, "new religions" or "alternative religions." To use the term cult here, is not to intend it as a pejorative, inflammatory word, but is used here simply to categorize certain religious or semi-religious groups in the world.

The English word cult comes from the Latin word cultus, which means "worship." In this sense it refers to a system of worship distinguishable from others. Of course, the modern usage is much more specific than the linguistic definition. Even though the word is often defined sociologically (a religious or semi-religious sect, or group whose members are almost entirely controlled by an individual or organization); for this study a religious definition would best serve.

Many have given insightful definitions. In his book, The Perilous Path of Cultism, author Orville Swenson, offers a definition that seems to best define the word, cult, in areligious sense. "a cult is religious group whose doctrines involve distortion of biblical truth, whose dedication and subservience to their domineering leaders is frequently excessive and blind, and whose attitudes, claims, practices, and teachings are divisive, creating an exclusive body of deviations from historical biblical Christianity).

DOCTRINAL CHARACTERISTICS OF TIIE CULTS

In that the largest and most influential cults are out of Christianity, it is important to understand their doctrinal characteristics that are common among cultism.

Denial of The Sole Authority of The Bible

Cult expert Anthony Hoekema has pointed out that when cults raise their own books or sets of books to the level of scripture, "God is no longer allowed to speak as He does in the Bible; He may now speak only as the sect deems proper. Thus, the Word of God is brought under the yoke of man."

New Revelation from God

Many cult leaders claim a direct pipeline to God It is interesting to note that the teachings of the cult often change as the groups need new "revelations" from Ascended Masters. In cults, greater credence is generally given to new revelations over past revelations (such as those found in the Bible). When there is a conflict between a new revelation versus an old revelation, the new revelation is always viewed as being authoritative.

Denial of the Trinity

Jehovah's Witnesses say the Trinity is a doctrine rooted in paganism and inspired by the devil with Jesus being a "lesser god". The Mormons speak of the Trinity, but they define it as three separate gods. Baha'is argue against the Trinity suggesting that Christian leaders do not understand their own scriptures. Most cults deny the Trinity by first denying the deity of Christ.

Denial of The Personality and Deity of The Holy Spirit

Many deny the deity of the Holy Spirit calling the Spirit an impersonal force of God. The "Moonies, for example, argue that the Holy Spirit is a female spirit and that together Jesus, and the Holy Spirit took the roles of "Second Adam" and "Second Eve." New Agers" try to equate the Holy Spirit with the "chi" force or "prana" energy of Eastern Religions.

Denial of the Full Deity of Christ

The Jehovah's Witnesses believe Jesus was created by the Father billions of years ago as the archangel Michael and is therefore a lessor god than the Father, who is "Almighty." The Mormons argue that Jesus was born as the first and greatest spirit child of the Heavenly Father and Heavenly Mother and was the spirit brother of Lucifer. The Masonic Lodge: "one of many ways to God." Edgar Cayce (a former Disciples of Christ Minister), a psychic, claimed Jesus was in his first incarnation Adam and in his thirtieth reincarnation became "the Christ" (The sinner and Savior are found in the same person). Oneness Pentecostals hold that Jesus alone is the Father, Son, and Holy Spirit. The Jesus of the UFO (New Age) cults is said to be half human and half alien, thereby accounting for his supernatural powers.

Devaluation of the Work of Christ

The work of Christ on the cross:

Mormonism; Brigham Young taught that some sins are so serious that the sinner must shed his own blood for atonement. Jehovah's Witnesses; "If Jesus had been God incarnate, the 'ransom payment' would have been way too much. Jesus' sacrifice only takes care of the sin we inherited from Adam, but we are on our own after that. We must 'work out' our own salvation."

Unification Church (Moonies); Spiritual redemption but not physical redemption;

Why not? "Because He was crucified by the Jews before He was able to meet His perfect mate, get married, and establish the Kingdom of Heaven on earth. Reverend Moon came here to complete what Jesus failed to accomplish."

The Real Issue Between Christians and Muslims (From a Christian perspective)

"Do Muslims and Christians worship the same God?" A question asked over and over.

In an article by Duane Liftin, former President of Wheaton College, Liftin addressed this question. The following, in part, is taken from his basic points. "This is a complex question in that all the words are loaded with ambiguity; how much sameness; what does 'worship' mean; what does the word Islam mean; how does a Muslim define God; and finally, which version of Christianity and which version of Islam. This then is the wrong question. If the goal is to compare these two religions one needs to shift his focus to a much more illuminating question: How does Christianity and Islam differ? With the answer to this question, one would be much better suited to address the sameness question."

Trinitarianism is often offered up as the core difference. Christianity embraces it, Islam does not. While accurate, this observation does not automatically locate the decisive issue. Neither the Old Testament faithful nor even the early Christians could have articulated orthodox Trinitarianism as it is understood today. Its doctrinal thesis was not formulated to well into the fourth century.

So, what is the difference? The decisive issue is quite simply; the Gospel-the Biblical account of what God has done, is doing, and will yet do through His Son-centered plan of redemption that reveals to us who the Creator truly is. Before the term Christian was applied to those who believed Jesus was the Son of God, early believers called themselves followers of "the Way". There is a clear reason for this. Christianity is about "the way" in which the Creator revealed now through His plan to be a loving heavenly Father and has graciously opened for his estranged, mutinous creatures to be reconciled to Him.

Quoting Liftin's brilliant summary; "According to the New testament, God sent his eternal Son into the world to embody that "way." From the Father's Son-centered redemptive purposes from "before the creation of the world" to the Son's creation of all that exists to the primeval promise of the Son's incarnation; through Israel's unfolding story in the Old Testament, all of which, Jesus said, was ultimately about him; to the plan's full flowering

162

in the birth, life, death, resurrection, ascension and exaltation of Jesus; to the plan's outworking ever since in the Sprit-empowered building of Christ's Kingdom; to the grand eschatological crescendo of the Son's second coming; all the way to the Son's final delivery of a fully redeemed and refashioned creation to the Father-through it all a TRIUNE God has been working His Son-centered, Spirit empowered plan of redemption!'

This fully elaborated story is what the Bible calls the gospel. It is this gospel that informs the gaping divide between Christianity and Islam. Christianity recognizes, embraces, and proclaims this Son-centered plan and the triune God it reveals to all who will hear. Islam repudiates this Son-centered plan and the divine trinity it reveals and substitutes a dramatically different proposal in its place. If the goal is to compare Christianity and Islam, this is the difference to grasp.

The "Sole Fide" Controversy

For the past six centuries a doctrine of "sole fide" (faith only) has divided Christian groups. Basically, the positions are:

1.We are justified by faith alone excluding all 'works." Most Protestant denominations take this position

2. Catholicism: In the General Council of Trent, The Catholic Church stated in Canon XIV on justification that, "If anyone saith, that man is truly absolved from his sins and justified; because that he assuredly believed himself to be absolved and justified; or that no one is truly justified but he who believes himself is justified, and that by this faith alone, absolution and justification are effected; let him be anathema (excommunicated)."

Contemporary evangelical theologian R.C. Sproul

writes, "The relationship between faith and good works is one that may be distinguished but never separated...if good works do not follow from our profession of faith, it is a clear indication that we do not possess justifying faith."

The Reformed formula is, "We are justified by faith alone but not by a faith that is alone." The position that justification is by faith alone has often been challenged with prompting antinomianism, in which saving faith need not be a type that will produce works of obedience to Christ, which is a view most who hold to 'sole fide' reject, including many authorities from the past and present in concurrence.

Martin Luther, who opposed antinomianism, is recorded as saying, "Works are necessary for salvation but they do not cause salvation; for faith alone gives life." Lutherans believe that individuals receive this gift of salvation through faith alone. Saving faith is the knowledge of, acceptance of, and trust in the promise of the Gospel. Even faith itself is seen as a gift of God, created in the hearts of Christians by the work of the Holy Spirit through the Word and baptism. Faith is seen as an instrument that receives the gift of salvation, not something that causes salvation. Thus, Lutherans reject the "decision theology" which is common among evangelicals. This writer, on one occasion, had this position stated by Lutheran Pastor friends regarding whether the Lutherans would support an area wide Billy Graham crusade. They refused with the "decision theology" doctrine objection as stated above, (basically, that unregenerate man cannot make this decision, but only by the Holy Spirit placing the gift of faith in man's head/heart can he be redeemed).

For Lutherans, justification provides the power by which the Christian can grow in holiness. Such improvement "comes in the believer only after he has become a new creature in Christ through Holy Baptism."

Because the Epistle of James emphasizes the importance of good works, Martin Luther sometimes referred to it as the "epistle of straw." Calvin on the other hand, while not intending to differ with Luther, described good works therefore or 'fruit' of faith. The Anabaptists tended to make a nominal distinction between faith and obedience.

There is a semantic component in the debate as well. Both Latin and English have two words to describe convictions: one is more "intellectual" and one carries implications of "faithfulness." Luther's supporters may have understood "salvation by faith alone" to mean "salvation by being faithful to Christ," while his opponents understood him to mean "salvation by intellectual belief in Christ."

Those who oppose the "faith only" theology of Luther and Reformed (Calvinism/Presbyterian) "faith only" theology of Calvin, suggest that while 'faith only' sounds good on the surface, and that it appears to be giving God all the glory, the fact of the matter is, God doesn't need their help. His wonderful scheme of redemption, which includes man's obedient response to the gospel of Christ, is already perfect. He doesn't forfeit His sovereignty by demanding that we believe, repent, confess and are baptized; nor does our response to His commands earn us a spot in heaven.

We are all saved by grace, as opposed to the meritorious works of the law. Baptism is neither a work of the 'law' nor a meritorious work, but a 'work of God' in us." They quote, "He quickened us by the gospel of His Son." ... " How did God make us alive? Peter tells us, 'by having purified your souls by your obedience to the truth for a sincere brotherly love ...... since you have been born again, not of perishable seed but of imperishable, through the living and abiding word of God"

Chapter 11

21st Century Religious Controversies
End time prophecies

Premillennialism

Premillennialism, in Christian eschatology, is the belief that Jesus will physically return to the earth to gather His saints before the Millennium, a literal thousand-year golden age of peace. This return is referred to as the Second Coming. The Doctrine is called "premillennialism" because it holds that Jesus' physical return to earth will occur prior to the inauguration of the Millennium. It is distinct from other Christian eschatology such as post-millennialism or amillennialism, which view the millennial rule as occurring either before the second coming, or as being figurative and non-temporal. For the last 150 years, the premillennial belief has been common in Evangelicalism.

Premillennialism is based upon a literal interpretation of Revelation 20:1-6 in the New Testament, which describes Jesus' reign in a period of a thousand years. It views this future age as a time of fulfilment for the prophetic hope of God's people as given in the Old Testament. Others, such as many in the Eastern Orthodox communion, claim that this passage of Revelation describes the present time, when Christ reigns in Heaven with the departed saints; such an interpretation views the symbolism of Revelation as referring to a spiritual battle rather than a physical battle on earth.

Historically, Christian "premillennialism' has also been

referred to as "chiliasm" (from chilias, the Greek word for thousand) or Millenarianism. The current terminology did not come into use until the mid-19th century. This is the period that coincided with an approach to Biblical studies that divorced eschatological textual interpretation from an historical context, where historical hermeneutics had Revelations being written to specific churches suffering persecution around the fall of the temple in 70A.D. and which traditional view was of no consequence to the new interpretation; likewise in interpreting Daniel, or the writings of The Apostle Paul. Coining the new word was almost entirely the work of Protestants, both Americans and British, prompted by the belief that the French and American Revolutions realized prophecies made in the books of Daniel and Revelation. Some have routinely accused Premillennialism of naive scholarship .... fortune telling."

Jewish Antecedents

The concept of a temporary earthly messianic kingdom at the messiah's coming was not an invention of Christianity. Instead it was a theological interpretation developed within the apocalyptic literature of early Judaism. In Judaism there was, during the Christian intertestamental period, a basic distinction between the Current age and the "age to come". The "age to come" was commonly viewed as a nationalistic Golden Age in which the hopes of the prophets would become a reality for the nation of Israel with a Jewish Messiah ruling the new age world.

Others have noted that when society is struggling with revolutions, terrorism, wars, and threats of nuclear annihilation (presently), people tend to intensify their religious beliefs reflecting a safe and victorious harbor beyond death where such threats can no longer exist; even in an earthly redeemed home where peace and prosperity would reign, as seen in historic Judaic eschatology i.e., forever earthly, or as in premillennialism; 1000 years earthly rein. R.H. Charles, in his commentary on the Book of Revelation, wrote, "Jewish eschatology must have developed the concept of an earthly temporary Messianic reign prior to the eternal state at the latest by 100 B.C."

Dispensational schools

Historic or Classic Pre-millennialism; meaning that the rapture of the church will occur after a period of tribulation (post tribulation) maintaining chiliasm, in that the church will be caught up to meet Christ in the air and then escort him to the earth to share in his literal thousand years rule. Charles Spurgeon and George Eldon Ladd were proponents.

Dispensational Pre-millennialism: Holds to the pre-tribulation return of Christ, which believes that Jesus will return to take up Christians into heaven by means of a rapture immediately before a seven-year worldwide tribulation. This will be followed by an additional return of Christ with his saints.

This school traces its roots to the 1830s and John Nelson Darby (1800-1882), an Anglican churchman and an early leader of the Plymouth Brethren. In the U.S. this form was propagated largely through the Scofield Reference Bible and on the academic level with Lewis Sperry Chafer's eight-volume Systematic Theology.

Some relegate Revelations' seven churches of Asia Minor to seven periods or dispensations of post resurrection history. They say, since 1900, we have been in the seventh and last period. A principle proponent of this position was Clarence Larkin, an American Baptist preacher in the mid-19th century. His ecological charts are still in use today.

More recently, works such as Hal Lindsey's "The Late Great Planet Earth and Tim Lahaye and Jerry Jenkins's Left Behind Series, have popularized Dispensationalism. Proponents also include: John MacArthur, Jerry Falwell, John Walvoord and Ray Comfort.

Recently another form has become popular: known as progressive dispensationalism; This view understands that an aspect of the eschatological kingdom presently exists but must wait for the millennium to be realized fully.

Christian denominations whose "Statements of Faith" reflect a pre-millennial position:

Most Baptist groups

International Pentecostal Holiness Church

Calvary Chapel

Evangelical Free Church of America

'Bible Churches', generally

Note: The Roman Catholic Catechism, pg. 676;…"that the millennium is understood as beyond history." The Missouri Synod (Lutheran); "When Christ returns new heavens and a new earth will be created."

A-millennialism

Proponents of A-millennialism interpret the millennium as being a symbolic period, which is consistent with the highly symbolic nature of the literary and apocalyptic genre of the book of Revelation, indicating that the thousand years represent (figuratively) God's rule over His creation or the church. They believe the Kingdom of God is presently the Church of Jesus Christ. They place emphasis on the present reign of King Jesus as Head of the church. Following are basic eschatological beliefs of A-millennialism:

Proponents' positions:

× Do not believe the Kingdom is primarily a Jewish Kingdom

× Do not believe that because of the unbelief of the Jews of Jesus day, Jesus postponed the establishment of the kingdom to the time of his future earthly millennial reign

× The Kingdom of God is both present and future

× Believe in 'inaugurated' eschatologies; a belief that significant eschatological events have already begun to happen while others still lie in the future

× The kingdom of god is both a present reality and a future hope

× Christians are already in the kingdom, and yet look forward to the full manifestation of that kingdom

Post-millennialism

Proponents of Post-millennialism believe that Christ will return after the millennium (the 'long period'), a Golden Age in which Christian ethics prosper, and that the world will gradually become Christianized through the mission of the church in preaching God's Word.

Post-millennialism expects that eventually the clear majority of men/women living will be saved. Increasing gospel success will gradually produce a time in history prior to Christ's return in which faith, righteousness, peace, and prosperity will prevail in the affairs of men and of nations. Then Jesus Christ will return visibly, bodily, and gloriously, to end history with the general resurrection and the final judgment after which the eternal order follows.

John Jefferson Davis notes that the post-millennial outlook was articulated by men like John Owens in the 17th century, Jonathan Edwards in the 18th century, and Charles Hodge in the 19th century. Davis argues that it was the dominant view in the 19th century but was eclipsed by the other millennial positions by the end of World War I due to the pessimism and disillusionment by wartime conditions.

During the Second Great Awakening of the 1830s, some expected the millennium to arrive in a few years. By the 1840s, however the great day had receded to the distant future, and post-millennialism became the religious dimension of the broader American middle-class ideology of steady moral and material progress.

Many post-millennials also adopt some form of preterism, which holds that many of the end times prophecies in the Bible have already been fulfilled. Several key post-millennials, however, did not adopt preterism with respect to the Book of Revelation, among them B.B. Warfield, Francis Nigel Lee, and Rousas John Rushdoony. Extreme Preterism holds that all end time prophecies have been fulfilled.

Fundamentalism
The following, in part, is attributed to Wikipedia.org

The term "fundamentalism" is sometimes applied to signify a counter-culture fidelity to a principle or set of principles, as in the pejorative term "market fundamentalism" applied to an exaggerated religious-like faith in the ability of unfettered laissez-faire or free market economic views or policies to solve economic and social problems. According to economist John Quiggin, the standard features of economic fundamentalist rhetoric" are "dogmatic" assertions and the claim that anyone who holds contrary views is not a real economist. Retired professor in religious studies Rodenck Hindery first lists positive qualities attributed to political, economic, or other forms of cultural fundamentalism. They include "vitality, enthusiasm, willingness to back up words with actions and the avoidance of facile compromise." Then, negative aspects are analyzed, such as psychological attitudes, occasionally elitist and pessimistic perspectives, and in some cases literalism.

Atheist

In December 2007, the Archbishop of Wales Barry Morgan criticized what he referred to as "atheistic fundamentalism", claiming that it advocated that religion has no substance and "that faith has no value and is superstitious nonsense. He claimed it led to situations such as councils calling Christmas "Waterval" schools refusing to put on nativity plays and crosses removed from chapels. Others have countered that some of these attacks on Christmas are urban myths, not all schools do nativity plays because they choose to perform other traditional plays like A Christmas Carol or The Snow Queen and because of rising tensions between various religions. Opening up public spaces to alternate displays than the Nativity scene is an attempt to keep government religion neutral.

Criticism

Many criticisms of fundamentalist positions have been offered. One of the most common is that some claims made by a fundamentalist group cannot be proven, and are irrational, demonstrably false, or contrary to scientific evidence. For example, some of these criticisms were famously asserted by Clarence Darrow in the Scopes Monkey Trial.

Sociologist of religion, Tex Sample, asserts that it is a mistake to refer to Muslim, Jewish, or Christian Fundamentalist. Rather, a fundamentalist's fundamentalism is their primary concern, over and above other denominational or faith considerations.

A criticism by Elliot N. Dorff:

To carry out the fundamentalist program in practice, one would need a perfect understanding of the ancient language of the original text, if indeed the true text can be discerned. As a result, it is impossible to follow the indisputable word of God; one can only achieve a human understanding of God's will.

Religious Fundamentalism

Both Calvin and Luther were Fundamentalist in theology; Both were 'reformers' of Catholic church abuses. Luther; "cannot change the smallest point of doctrine". Billy Graham represented "neo-evangelicalism; he parted with Fundamentalists because he cooperated with other Christians.

Fundamentalism can be traced to all religious groups in history. Early civilization created 'gods' so that the tribal leaders could claim their gods spoke to them and no one else and thus demanding tribal obedience and control and consequently negating any 'modernism' trends among the people.

This report, in part, is attributed to wikipedia.org.

Biological Evolutionism and Creationism

Dr. Gene Hwang, born in 1950 in Tainan, Taiwan, is a retired professor of mathematics at the National Chung Cheng University in Taiwan. He is also professor emeritus at Cornell University where he taught and did research in statistics and probability. As young man he believed life began by evolutionary processes. But later changed his view about his work and religious beliefs.

In a recent interview, Dr. Hwang spoke of this spiritual and academic transformation: "Does your faith conflict with your secular views?" He replied, "Not at all. In recent years I have provided mathematical support for scientists who study gene function. The study of genetics provide insight into the mechanisms of life."

"What do you think of the Bible?" Again, "I was impressed by its account of how the earth was prepared for human life. The six creative periods described in Geneses, albeit in simple language, seemed to fit the facts-unlike ancient mythologies. Still, for many years I did not commit to belief in a creator."

"Later, though, your viewpoint changed. Why was that?" Dr. Hwang, "The more I thought about the origin of life, the more I became convinced that the first living thing must have been complex. For example, it had to be able to reproduce, which requires genetic information and a mechanism for accurately replicating that information. Also, even the simplest living cells need molecular machines for building all the parts of a new cell, as well as the means to harness and direct energy. How could such complex mechanisms assemble randomly from nonliving matter? As a mathematician, I could not accept that assumption. It asks far too much of random processes-an insight that fills me with awe for the Creator's wisdom."

"Give an example of that wisdom." "Consider reproduction. Some organisms, such as amoebas, don't have male and female counterparts. These single-cell microbes simply make a copy of their genetic information and divide-a process called asexual reproduction. Most animals and plants, however, reproduce sexually, combining genetic information from male and female parents." "Why is sexual reproduction remarkable?"

"Why would a system of reproduction in which one organism simply divides into two-and has done this very well for who knows how long-develop into a system in which two things combine to form one? The mechanisms required to take half the genetic information from the male and half from the female and combine then are immensely complex, presenting a huge problem to evolutionary biologists. In my view, gender-based reproduction points unequivocally to the mind of God."

Darwin's Theory of Evolution and Religion
CONTROVERSY

Most religious groups espouse Creationism over against Darwin's Evolutionist theory.

When defining religious conservative orthodoxy one invariably also defines the character of philosophical/political orthodoxy; the same with rigid liberalism; both religious and philosophical. In both is found a stubborn belief in absolutes.

The fundamentalist Protestant and Catholic, especially those among evangelical and Bible churches, argue that God created all things in seven 24-hour days; that the earth is around 6000 years old (Irish bishop, James Ussher's earth age of 6000 years calculation).

Citing testimony during the Bryan/Darrow "monkey" trial, Mr. Brian stated, "My impression is they (the seven days) were periods, but I would not attempt to argue against anybody who wanted to believe in literal days." A few years ago, Jerry Falwell responded, "Bryan lost the respect of Fundamentalists when he subscribed to the idea of periods of time for creation rather than the twenty-four-hour days."

Besides the controversy between the 24 hour believers and the progressive liberals who dismiss Creationism out right, there is an ever-increasing controversy within the ranks of conservative Protestants; Orthodox Creationism vs. Theistic evolution.

Theistic Evolution; those who accept fossil evidence and a more metaphorical interpretation of the 'days' of Genesis, but who still insist that species were intelligently designed by God and not the products of evolution.

Initially most theistic evolutionists believed that God guided the evolutionary process to specific ends. However, as the Darwinian view of the undirected nature of evolution gradually solidified in the scientific community, defenders of theistic evolution increasingly disowned the idea of 'guided' evolution. Today leading proponents of theistic evolution insist that Darwinian evolution is an undirected process and that not even God knows what the process will produce with certainty.

Kenneth Miller of Brown University, author of the popular book, Finding Darwin's God" (which is used in many Christian colleges), insists that evolution is an undirected process to achieve any particular result-including the development of human beings. Miller did say that God knew that the undirected process of evolution was so wonderful that it could create some sort of rational creature capable of praising

Baptism; a Dividing Issue

If there is one common dividing issue among religious groups, it would be baptism; its mode, meaning and effect. All major religions, in one way or another deal with baptism.

Catholicism;
(quoting from their New Catechism, pgs. 348-360)

"The Church does not know of any means other than baptism that assures ently into eternal beatitude." ... "all who can be baptized are 'reborn of water and the Spirit." ... "God has bound salvation to the Sacrament of Baptism, but he himself is not bound by his sacrament." ... "effects of baptism: purification from sins, and new birth in Christ. "..."By baptism ALL sins are forgiven, original sin and all personal sins, as well as all punishment for sin."

"For those who die before their baptism, their explicit desire to receive it, together with repentance for their sins, and charity, assures them of salvation." ... "Every man who is ignorant of the Gospel of Christ and of his Church, but seeks the truth and does the will of God in accordance with his understanding of it, can be saved."

The Catholic Church practices infant and children's baptism as "coming to Christ through the gift of holy baptism." The form of baptism: Affusion ("to pour on") Who can baptize? ... . "in case of necessity, anyone, even a non-baptized person, with the required intention, can baptize, by using the Tlinitarian baptismal formula."

Lutheranism;
"The purpose of baptism is to save." (Luther's Large

Catechism)

Presbyterianism:

According to their "Reformed Theology"; baptism is not necessary for salvation. Infants? "Baptism is a matter of faith; with infants, the parents' faith; with adults, their own faith."*

Methodism,

"Baptism is part of the journey of salvation."*

Episcopalian:

"Baptism is receiving the individual into the household of faith."

*also maintains a link between baptism and regeneration.

Baptists, Anabaptists, and Evangelical Protestants recognize baptism as an outward sign of an inward reality following an individual believer's experience of forgiving grace. Do not believe baptism is necessary for salvation.

Churches of Christ, Christian Churches, and...

Jehovah's Witnesses, Christadelphians, and the LDS Church are but a few who espouse baptism as necessary for salvation. Most of these groups consistently teach that in baptism a believer surrenders his life in faith and obedience to God, and that God "by the merits of Christ's blood, cleanses one from sin and truly changes the state of the person from an alien to a citizen of God's Kingdom. Baptism is not a human work, it is the place where God does the work that only God can do." Thus, they see baptism as a passive act of faith rather than a meritorious work; "it is a confession that a person has nothing to offer God."

Full Gospel churches:

Separated from the Baptists in 1994; maintain mostly Baptist theology concerning water baptism. However, primary emphasis is placed upon Holy Spirit Baptism and regenerational Double Blessing theology. They cite: 1st Blessing; baptism for the forgiveness of past sins. 2nd Blessing; "reaching 2nd blessing is a growing state of 'sinless perfection; that takes tremendous work to accomplish-a Spirit filled life."

Judaism

Baptism has always been part of Jewish theology. Today, it is administered in proselytizing ceremonies wherein the proselyte "comes from darkness to light." Baptism is the cleansing of the person from the impurities of idolatry, and the restoration of the purity of a new born man. Baptismal purification fits their regenerational theology; a state in which the convert will share in the Kingdom of God; for most Jews, an eternal blissful life in a new Messianic Kingdom on earth. "Salvation" is not a word used in Jewish Baptism or theology.

Islam

Muslims do not celebrate baptism in the Christian sense. Islam challenges the authority of baptism by citing the Quran's declaration that participation in the religion is itself the baptism of Allah. Baptism is based upon cleansing oneself with water before praying, and other ritualistic cleansing ceremonies; "appropriate Muslim behavior."

Premillennialism and Modern Charlemagne

The Fourth Reich, could easily be the title of a recent booklet, "Germany and the Holy Roman Empire" published by the Philadelphian Church of God, an off-shoot of Herbert Armstrong's Church of God International. Adventist churches have long espoused eschatological (end time) belief in:

1. Jesus' immanent return (2nd Coming)

2.The 'premillennial' return of Christ and His subsequent 1000-year reign on earth.

The booklet's theme is predicated on the proposition that the Anti-Christ of the Book of Revelation historically has been:

1. The Roman Catholic Pope and the Holy Roman Catholic Church in general.

2. That in modem times (today) the Anti-Christ will take the form of a coalition between the Roman Church and Germany, thus forming a super state like the vast area reigned over by Charlemagne (Charles the Great) 1300 years ago (the First Reich). Once in place, this 'Super state" would bring the rest of the world under its control. It would be the battle for control of the greater 'World state.'

Jews were not always maligned either under Charlemagne's reign or under Hitler's Third Reich. Both placed Jewish economists in financial positions while keeping this secret. Both acknowledged the alleged 'Jewish money mastery." But for Hitler, the pure Teutonic blood racing through his Nordic veins trumped whatever affection he had for Jewish economic know how. To illustrate the reality, the Jewish WWII genocide death toll, including shootings and the camps, was between 5.2 and 5.8 million, roughly half of Europe's Jewish population. Why did Hitler hate the Jews? One; latent and sometimes overt strong antisemitism in Europe. Two, he believed the Jews led the revolutionaries and Socialists in starting and losing WWI.

The booklet writer suggests this connection: The First Reich, ruled over by Charles, had to "wade through a sea of blood" to achieve his goal of ruling Europe, while the Third Reich ruler, Hitler, also 'waded through a sea of blood' in his attempt to rule Europe and eventually the world." This, they believe was a preview of the coming political beast that will initiate a nuclear holocaust, irrespective of the present far east-west's tensions. To the premillennial this, then, would usher in Christ's return.

With Germany and France, the new key players, it will come down to the nation that controls the money will reign supreme."
Note: The Second Reich is said to be the inner period between
the World Wars, 1919-1933.

This 'End Times' eschatological theory continues: "As always, there is the monetary aspect of this new Super State" with both Germany and France the key players. The nation that controls the money will reign supreme. As long as the new EU monetary authority looks, sounds, smells and acts as the German monetary authority the Germans are prepared to accept an apparent cession of national monetary authority. A Trojan horse is a term used while describing this as a cloak for German ambitions. The bigger question remains: in the new empire of Charlemagne, WHO WILL PLAY CHARLEMAGNE? "

Hitler, at times, demonstrated a twisted interest in extreme cult worship. This faux interest in religion and his crafting a war time agreement with the Roman Church, the Church accommodated him by looked the other way. Now, the theory goes, they again will consolidate power with the Roman Catholic Church.

How could the Roman Church accommodate the blood bath of Hitler's satanic quest as well as her accommodation through the first and second Reich"?

This then, is one of the many postulates of premillennialism eschatology. How similar it is to Jewish eschatology whereby a Jewish Messiah will come as a conquering king and reign over an ageless economic utopia.

Premillennialists have a difficult time defending their position when major proponents continue to wrongly date the 'second coming' of Jesus, and their misnaming histories' "bad guys" as the Ant-Christ.

The book's author concludes; "the Fourth Reich has arrived whether we realize it or not."

Chapter 12

Scientology
L Ron Hubbard Founder, 1911-1986.

Hubbard, a Nebraska native, died from a stroke. He had penned 200 novels. Education: Claimed a B.A. from George Washington University, but flunked freshman physics; was placed on probation; left school never to return.

Hubbard had no medical background, but as his critics note, that did not stop him from claiming that because of applying his techniques, "arthritis vanishes, myopia gets better, heart illness decreases, asthma disappears, stomachs function properly ...(Source: Dianetics MSMH, page 46), as well as many other claims including raising the dead. Dianetics: His most influential work. Claim: Dianetics is the ultimate development of the mind of human beings.

Beyond this was his study of the human spirit. Scientology: "the road from there (Dianetics) to ultimate freedom.". Church structure: Like the Catholic Church. Size: 3500 churches and organizations, with 8M people in 100 countries.' People: Tom Cruise, Kristy Alley, Mime Rogers, John Travolta. These and other adherents assemble frequently in Hollywood's seven story "Celebrity Centre."

Doctrine: One must ascribe to it. Thetan; an immortal Spirit, mankind; both good and divine, no sin nature; man fell into matter, not sin; existed before creation. Reincarnation: at death, the Thetan enters a new human body. Every new body has accumulated countless engrains (sensory impressions) after trillions of years of their existence.

Mind: Two parts. Analytic and Reactive.

Analytic: Rational

Reactive: The place of stored memories; each experience causes an "engrain'. These 'impressions' cause emotional and other kinds of pain plus inappropriate behavior.

Salvation: "Attained through increasing one's spiritual awareness." How then can man be delivered from the bondage to the Reactive mind? According to Hubbard, the solution to the problem is through finding and neutralizing engrains. To do that one must use an auditor; (Scientology's process called auditing).

Auditing: (Administered by a minister or minister in training) Auditors receive commissions, usually 10% on their books and courses) Auditing involves: "free personality tests" which they call the Oxford Capacity Analysis" test which its critics claim has nothing to do with Oxford University. It takes a perfect score which again critics claim on the test it is impossible to get a perfect score. The "free stress test" will prove you need their help (with the aid of U serious and scientific-looking machine). The claim: "The E-meter claim: assists in improving the health and bony functions of anyone."

Scientology's internal vocabulary: a range of thought stopping phrases; terms used specifically to try to stop you from thinking further about a subject. The phrases fall into two categories: "Entheta" as describing something as being bad for your spiritual wellbeing. "Suppressive" as describing a person being bad for you. 'TRs": (Training Routines) marketed as ways to help you communicate. Critics describe them as being hypnotic drills to· plant the seeds of mind control. "Free"; Means to pass the 'audit; to remain 'free', one must enroll in subsequent courses called "eight dynamics of life." Total costs for all eight: $200,000-$400,000 (all commissioned to the "Auditor") Suppressive Person: one who leaves Scientology. Leah Remini (who left) said, "It becomes your mother, father, your everything."

L.Ron Hubbard held as being utterly infallible and therefore his every word should be followed without question. David Miscavige: Present day global head of Los Angeles based Scientology.

Reference materials: The Challenge of the Cults, -Ron Rhodes, Zondervan

Web: Scientology-Cult .com, portrait of a ponzi man;

The Kingdom of the Cults, Walter Martin, Bethany Fellowship, 1977, Wikipedia; CULTS

Religion in Congress, 2017

From the Christian Standard-
Pew Research Center, "Faith on the Hill" 1/3/2017

While the share of American adults who describe themselves as Christians declined for decades, the new 115th U.S. Congress is about as Christian as it was in the early 1960s.

91 percent: Members of the 115th Congress who identify as Christians.

95 percent: Members of the 87th Congress (1961-62) who identified as Christians.

291: Republican members of Congress who identified as Christians. (out of 293 total); The other two Republicans identify as Jews.

194: Democratic members who identify as Christians .out of 242

28: Democrat members who identify as Jews. Other

Democrats identify as Buddhists (3), Hindus (3), Unitarian-Universalist (1),

"Unaffiliated" or "none" (1) Ten members declined to state their religious affiliation.

Religion in public school

When applied to current challenges, one must include the debate and divisions over the issue of religion in the public schools.

Charles Haynes, a senior scholar at the First Amendment Center, and the director of the center's Religious Freedom Education Project, in a recent article in "A Desert News Faith", gives insight into a small part of history and tensions intensifying the school/religion debate. In part, he said the following: In 1844, 20 people died in Philadelphia in that which was labeled the "Bible Riots." An issue arose over which version of the Bible would be used in the public-school classrooms; the Protestant King James Version or the Catholic Douay Rheims Version, used by the new Irish Catholic immigrants.

The present conflict, although not as inflammable as that which led to that deathly violence and 50 years ago to a U.S. Supreme Court's decision; a decision known today as the Schempp Decision, continues to have troubling consequences.

Fifty years ago, in Abington High School (Pennsylvania), a 17-year-old student sat quietly reading from a borrowed Koran while another student was customarily reading from the King James Bible in the class's daily devotional. That which seemed to have been a larger issue was that when the students, again as customary, stood to recite the Lord's Prayer, Schempp remained seated. Young Schempp later said, "I knew I could get in trouble." Haynes wrote, "If people want to know when religion left the public schools, it was a long time ago, when people couldn't agree on sectarian teaching."

David Doty, Superintendent of the Canyon School District in Sandy, Utah made the following observations, " ... alternatives to opt out of a class on the Bible as literature or a choral group performing a religious composition and take another comparable course takes special planning and funding; not a viable option in many funds strapped Districts. I have always felt that being able to include religion in the appropriate context and parameters in public schools is critical in saving public schools." Doty added, "more students are fleeing public schools for private schools, home schools, and charter schools because of value issues. I think that if public schools persist in a hard-fast wall of Separation of Church and State, it does send the wrong message."

Religion and Education

Cynthia Allen, a columnist with the Ft. Worth Star-Telegram addressed the impact of formal education, or the lack of it, has on American religiosity:

She wrote, "When President Obama made his now famous 2008 remark that working-class voters frustrated by their economic circumstances "cling to guns or religion," his subject was clear; religion is a crutch for the poor and uneducated.

In fairness, the former president was articulating what has been the conventional wisdom about faith in modem America-that it is, as Karl Marx described, an "opiate for the masses" and that an increase in education and scholarship erodes belief. To a degree that last statement has merit. In the U.S., studies indicate that adults with higher levels of education are more likely than their counterparts with less education to identify as atheists or agnostics. Similarly, college graduates are less likely to pray daily or to say that religion is of prime importance in their lives, when compared to people with only a high school diploma or less.

But a new analysis by the Pew Research Center challenged the notion that more education leads to less faith and shows that faith and education in many cases are not inversely related. Indeed, among certain religious groups, higher degrees of education are associated with more religiosity, not less. This is particularly true with Christianity.

Pew's research looked at data from several different studies and found that while educated people are generally less likely to believe in God (believers; 83 percent of college graduates versus 92 percent of people with only a high school degree), that difference all but disappeared among the various sects of Christianity. The relationship between education and religious practices-attending services-is even more fascinating because it turns conventional thinking about faith and education on its head. When it comes to church attendance, for example, college graduates are more likely than their less-educated peers to fill the pews. Only Americans with no affiliation and those who identify as Jewish tend to show a decrease in belief and faith practice as education rises. The Pew analysts do not speculate as to why these patterns have emerged, but even their dispassionate writing cannot completely disguise their surprise.

Christianity in the U.S. has been on decline for decades,

and the number of Americans who do not identify with any organized religion is growing-a reality many have attributed to progressive thought. Why then are we finding that intellectual enlightenment will in many cases enhance religiosity and not hinder it? Knowledge, properly understood, is the acceptance of the vastness of the universe and how little about it we are capable of mastering. What we have left with is faith.

Religion and Music

After the spoken word, music has played and does play the major role in religious worship of all the world's major religions. In the study of one tradition, other traditions are found so ingrained, that it is very difficult to identify originality.

Following are brief sketches of historical religious music as expressed in worship by major faiths:

Christianity

Christianity began as a small persecuted Jewish sect. At first there was little break with the Jewish faith; Christians still attended synagogues and the Second Temple in Jerusalem just as Jesus had done, and presumable still carried on the same musical traditions in their separate meetings. (the name Christian was not used until later). The only record of communal song in the Gospels is the last meeting of the disciples before the crucifixion. Outside the Gospels, there is a reference to Paul's encouraging the Ephesians and Colossians to use psalms, hymns and spiritual songs.

Later in Bithynia the Christians were reported as gathering before sunrise and repeating antiphonally "a hymn to Christ as to God." Antiphonal psalmody is the singing or musical playing of psalms by alternating groups of performers. This method originated in the services of the ancient Israelites. According to the historian Socrates of Constantinople, its introduction into Christian worship was due to Ignatius of Antioch (died in 107), who in a vision had seen the angels singing in alternate choirs.

The use of musical instruments in early Christian music seems to have been frowned upon. In the late 4th or early 5th century St. Jerome wrote that a Christian maiden ought not even to know what a lyre or flute is like, or to what use it is put. The introduction of organ music is traditionally believed to date from the time of the Papacy of Pope Vitalian in the 7th century.

The term 'Mass' was first used to note a form of music that sets out the Eucharistic liturgy (in Catholic, Anglican and Lutheran churches) to music. Such masses can be sung acapella, for the human voice alone, or they can be accompanied by instrumental obbligatos up to a full orchestra. Many of the masses, especially the later ones, were never intended to be performed during the celebration of an actual masses. Most liturgical churches refer to their 'masses' written in English, as Communion services.

In the middle ages, chants were most common among Western Christianity. After falling into disuse in the 16-18th centuries the practice was revived and in still in use in European and American churches. The Gregorian chant is the main tradition of Western plainchant. The musical form originated in early Monastic life.

Chants become best-selling album, an AP headline in May 2017, with the story of members of the Priestly Fraternity of St. Peter, a Catholic order formed in 1988, recently releasing an album, "Requiem", singing a traditional Latin funeral Mass. The album quickly became the best-selling album on Amazon. The director was quoted, "To think that this music is the same sound, the same melodies that someone would have heard even a thousand years ago at the death of a loved one. There's something transcendent I find about the music. It's very peaceful, very calming, and very conducive it seems to prayer." One of the Seminarians was quoted; "From the first time you step into the seminary, we are constantly being formed in Gregorian chant, which is part and parcel with the mode of worship that we use here in the seminary."

Protestant Music

In most Protestant congregations, music forms have changed dramatically over the last 30 years. From traditional hymns, organ and piano to guitars, drums, brass, and keyboards, miked 'praise team', theater style lighting and large screens spelling out the words, (often with multiple repetition of the words), as the music's intensity rises.

Those who still prefer the traditional style services, i.e. hymns vs praise songs; piano vs. guitars/drums, claim that the 'new' music is intended to incite emotions alone, a limited expression; while traditional " hymns, psalms and spiritual songs" add critical Biblical education and edification along with praise and celebration.

Some Protestant church groups, in their corporate worship, choose to sing acapella (without musical instruments). At a recent Pepperdine University symposium, "The Ascending Voice II, a gathering of 500 music directors of the Churches of Christ, a conservative body of some 8500 congregations (Not to be confused with

The United Church of Christ) again studied the declining roll of church music. The leader was quoted; " many congregations sing fewer-and in some cases none-of what he described as "the great Protestant four part hymns or even the Stamps-Baxter songs, which used to be the more popular style of our song repertory." .. "Instead they rule moving quickly to praise songs. Thus, we are producing a generation that, that if they are not into school music, may have never looked at a piece of written music and have never learned to sing four-part harmony."

One of the married couple added; "It seems we spend 50 percent of our worship time singing, but there's almost no education on how the process works, how to read music, what music is good for singing ... "

"Acapella" churches: Some Anglican, Eastern Orthodox Churches, Church of God in Christ, Primitive Baptists, some Reformed Churches and the Churches of Christ.

Music: Islamic Tradition

Music in the Islamic world is to express and encapsulate the most important concept of the Qur'an: tawhid, or "unity with God."

There are various devices that Muslims use express tawhid, but in sum these characteristics can be described as forms of abstraction: "Since tawhid teaches that God cannot be identified with any object or being from nature, He cannot be musically associated with sounds that arouse psychological or kinesthetic correspondences to beings, events, objects, or ideas within nature" (al Faruqi, 1986). Thus, Islamic music must be nonprogrammatic and must not create events that would evoke or express extra-musical ideas that are associated with human emotions, human problems, or earthly-musical occurrences: "We refer to the saying of the Prophet in which he condemned artists who 'ape' the creation of God: in their afterlife they will be ordered to give life to their works and will suffer from their incapacity to do so" (Burckhardt, 1987).

Such abstraction can also be readily perceived in Islamic art "arabesque" art, for example, which never depicts images of humans, animals or the natural world, but instead focuses solely on the creation of patterns. The point of Islamic music is to avoid focus on worldly concerns, which are of no value and only distracts man from focus on God:" Islamic art corroborates a void with abstract forms, instead of ensnaring the mind and dragging it into some imaginary world, thus detaching the consciousness from the inward 'idols.' In other words, man without images of himself can remain more pure and uninhibited from contemplating God.

Hindu Music

Hindu music is music created for or influenced by Hinduism. It includes Hindu classical music, Kirwan, Bajan and other musical genres. Ragas are a common form of Hindu music in classical India. The most common Hindu bajan in North Cat India is "Om Jai Jagdish Hare." The names of Gods are religiously chanted, often including Vishnu and his incarnations, Shiva and the Goddesses (Parvati, Shakti, Vaishnodevi).

A Bhajan is a Hindu devotional song, often of ancient origin. Bhajans are often simple songs of lyrical language expressing emotions of love for the divine, whether for a single God/Goddess, or any number of divinities. Many bhajans feature several names and aspects of the chosen deity, especially in the case of Hindu sahasranamas, which list a divinity's 1008 names. Hindus are even said to have achieved Moksha (the end of the life and death cycle with the soul's freedom) through devoting music to God.

Buddhism and Music

In Buddhism, chanting is the traditional means of preparing the mind for meditation, especially as part of formal practice (either in the lay or monastic context). Some forms of Buddhism also use chanting for ritualistic purposes.

A Buddhism chant is a form of musical verse or incantation, in some ways analogous to Hindu, Christian or Jewish recitations. These exist in just about every part of the Buddhist world, from the Wats in Thailand to the Tibetan Buddhist temples in India and Tibet. Almost every school has some tradition of chanting associated with it, regardless of being Theravada or Mahayana.

The most popular chant is the Buddhabhivadana (Preliminary Reverence for the Buddha). The most common bodily position for chanting is sitting with legs crossed and hands cupped upwards over the chest.

The Mind Sciences

Phineas Parkhurst Quimby was born in New Lebanon, New Hampshire, in 1802. As an adult he developed a keen knack for meta physics. Ultimately, he is the father of all the mind sciences. Quimby would often use his metaphysical techniques to heal people, whether they could pay for it. He eventually committed his theories to writing, producing some ten volumes of manuscripts in which he discussed religion, disease, spiritualism, clairvoyance, science, error and truth. His writings have never been published. In his writings he espoused the metaphysical idea that physical diseases are caused by wrong thinking or false beliefs. Disease is merely an "error" created "not by God, but by man." Eliminate false beliefs, and the chief culprit for disease is thereby removed, yielding a healthy body. These false beliefs are remedied Quimby believed by "the Christ."

Quimby's metaphysics spawned several important movements. The term "New Thought" surfaced as a way of describing some of the metaphysical groups that emerged from his thinking. New Thought author, Horatio Dresser, commented, "The 'old thought' was undeniably pessimistic; it dwelt on sin, emphasized the darkness and misery of the world; the distress and the suffering."

New Thought Theology:

God: A pantheistic God, called "Universal life Force," "Infinite Idea," "All is one and One is God," "Presence" indicating a nebulous concept of God.

Man: Is viewed as divine with unlimited potential and readily available. Sin: no real sin; a succumbing to the illusory world of matter.

Death: So called death is an entry into the fourth dimension of life, and our journey is from glory to glory, from wisdom to wisdom, ever onward upward and Godward. ...... no end to the glory which is man.

The New Thought concept has spawned three major movements: Christian Science, the United Church of Religious Science, and the Unity School of Christianity. In that it represents the basic beliefs of all three, Christian Science, with the largest following, will be studied here. These movements are collectively known as the "mind sciences."

Recently, I was having a cup of coffee at a local Starbucks. As only one chair was available, taking that seat would place me next to a lovely young lady who was both drinking coffee and working on her laptop. (The following line is for my wife's perusal). I reluctantly sat down and before long we were engaged in theological chit chat.

As I was having a difficult time hearing or understanding her, with all the café noise, she quietly pulled out paper and pen and proceeded to write and give to me her 'theology'. New Thought theology came to mind as I read the following:

'The Real Christ will walk on earth, <u>with you</u>. Faker Christ will have apparitions in the sky. Real love can't be mimicked. Real Christ will tell you what his Real name was… Love, Kelsea, (I was Sarah)"

On a foot note, she scribed, *"the meek shall inherit the earth."*

To my readers, let me hear from you if you have some insight here. Her belief system would reflect what?

Christian Science

Mary Baker Patterson: Eddy was the founder. She held that in 1866 after reading Matt. 9: 1-8 she had an almost miraculous healing of a severe injury. From that time on she sought knowledge re the science of this healing. Her findings are in her own words, "a scientific system of divine healing." In 1875 her principle work was published, Science and Health with a key to the Scriptures. She set up the Church of Christ, Scientist at Boston in 1879, and later establishing there in 1892 a mother church, The First Church of Christ, Scientist.

Eddy derived most of her theology from Quimby. She

had become interested in him because of his growing fame as a healer. Eddy was not an original thinker but took what Quimby developed and popularized it in a new movement which she called Christian Science. She became acquainted with Quimby when she sought treatment for spinal inflammation. She claims she became healed because of Quimby' s care. This resulted in her studying and even teaching Quimby' s metaphysical system. Historically her "cure" was short lived as the pain soon returned. Yet she still believed that the answer to her suffering was the metaphysical teaching of Quimby.

Nine years after Quimby died in 1875, Eddy published her book, Science and health with key to the Scriptures. Only in passing did she mention Quimby. Yet she set forth the principles she had learned from Quincy. She spoke of her ideas as new "revelation" even though it was 'derived' revelation. This plagiarism later became public. While denying stealing her ideas from Quimby, a New York Times article published in 1904 thoroughly documented it. Eddy rebutted that she herself had discovered metaphysical healing techniques after she had fallen on icy pavement. She claimed that she had been given only three days to live by medical authorities but was restored to health through metaphysical techniques she had discovered. The doctor who had treated her, Dr. Alvin M. Cushing, contradicted her claim, stating in an affidavit that she had not been in critical condition or near death, and he knew of no such miracle of which Eddy spoke.

The theology starts with the idea that God is the only mind. A sharp distinction is drawn between the real and the apparent but unreal. It teaches that all evil and error is to be overcome based on its unreality. Part of the rule is found in John 8:32, "Ye shall know the truth and the truth shall make you free." The practice of Christian Science is both a mental and a spiritual discipline. The practitioner must prepare for the healing ministry-healing of all evils, not sickness alone-by living the genuine Christian life. Mrs. Eddy died in 1910.

By the time Eddy died there were about one million people attending Christian Science churches. By the mid-1960s the church membership began to decline and that continues to this day. Losses of membership took its toll on its TV and newspaper media. In 1993 the church began selling off its media network. Another controversy erupted in the 1990s because of Bliss Knapp's book, Destiny of the Mother Church, which declared Mary Baker Eddy to be equal to and a successor of Jesus Christ. The book essentially deified Eddy. Many, even in the Christian Science movement, considered this heresy. However. the Knapps had stipulated that $90 million would be left to the church on the condition that this book would be published and then prominently displayed in Christian Science reading rooms across the country. As it turns out the church finally received about half of the ninety million, while the rest had been quietly pledged to Stanford University and the Los Angeles Museum of Art. Many church members resigned over the affair.

Today there are 2300 branch churches in more than 60 countries, 1600 in the United States. It is estimated that the church now has fewer than 250,000 members

Chapter 13

Faith of the Founding Fathers

There has been much discussion in recent years as whether this nation is a "Christian nation" or not. Adding to the discussion is the question as to the faiths or religions of the Founding fathers; many insisting that the great majority were Christians. But history tells a different story.

However, it must be noted that the period of history in which this study is cast found most citizens of the new world were Christians with faith roots planted by their European ancestors who had arrived mainly as a result of religious persecution. By the 1750s the religious fires were burning low. As a result, the Political leaders of nation's formative years may themselves been spiritually weakened by this condition. It must also be noted that The First Great Awakening, this nation's first great religious revival, began by many accounts at the beginning of the second half of the eighteenth century.

Following is a list of these early patriots and their faith...

Generally, it is believed that most were either Deists or Unitarians; (Impersonal Providence).

Thomas Paine; a protegee of Benjamin Franklin. Author, Age of Reason, Pamphleteer, his manifestoes; "I disbelieve them all (creedal statements); and Christianity; a fable.

George Washington; never declared himself a Christian. Championed the cause of freedom from "religious importance and compulsion."

John Adams, 2nd President; Orthodox Unitarian. Faced

pressure from father to become a clergyman. He called some of these clergymen, "absolute dunces." "Best if there were no religions in the world."

Thomas Jefferson; 3rd President; author, Declaration of Independence. "Not a young man who will not die a Unitarian." He called the book of Revelation, "the ravings of a maniac." He saw the Mysticisms of Plato as a system used by the Christian Priesthood, to build up an artificial system whereby their 'order' would profit, gain power and pre-eminence ...... "that nonsense can never be explained."

James Madison; 4th President; Father of the Constitution; "Religious bondage shackles and debilitates the mind and unfits it for noble enterprise." ... claimed to be a Christian Deist.

Ethan Allen; (captured Fort Ticonderago), pursued the war of Independence; a non-Christian Deist. "Jesus Christ was not God."

Benjamin Franklin; considered a Deist; "some doubts as to His (Jesus) divinity" "Jesus system"; various currupting changes; but never studied it."

James Monroe; Episcopalian, but "a non-Christian Deist."

John Quincy Adams; 6th President; Orthodox Christian

Alexander Hamilton; Revolutionary General; author of the Federalist papers, Treasury Secretary, called, "very orthodox" Christian. Requested communion while dying on the field; Aaron Burr dual.

John Hancock; declaration signer; governor of Mass. President of Congress; very little information on any religious affiliation or belief.

John Jay; orthodox Christian

Daniel Webster: U.S. Senator; Christian Deist; "good Christians make good citizens ... Bible a book that teaches responsibility, dignity, and equality." Christian

Deists; historians name Thomas Jefferson and George Washington Orthodox Christians; Calvinists; Sam Adams and John Jay; Elias Boudinot wrote, "The Second Coming of Christ", Patrick Henry distributed religious tracks while 'riding around'.

Historical Notes

"In God we trust" (Pledge of Allegiance) inserted in 1856. The Treaty of Tripoli (1797); by unanimous vote declared, "the government of the United States is not in any sense founded on the Christian religion." (There were three abstentions) In 1805 the treaty was amended without the statement.

The Encyclopedia Britannica summarized in an article on early national leaders; "Most were either religious rationalists or Unitarian. It appears that some of the Founding Fathers were orthodox (right believing) Christians. They sought divine assistance. Most of these had 'old world' religious faiths: Anglican, Presbyterian, Congregational, Roman Catholic, Lutheran and Friends affiliations." Many leaders evolved into non-Christian Deism, Christian Deism, or Orthodox Christians.

Deism influenced most of the Founders. They opposed barriers to moral improvement and social justice; stood for national inquiry with skepticism about dogma, mystery, and religious toleration; advocated for universal education, freedom of the press, and separation of Church and State. They embraced liberal ideas remarkable for their time."

History of Religious Texts

Sacred texts form the cornerstone of a religion, instilling

law, character and spirituality in its people; some are narratives of historical figures of the faith. A text might be viewed as the unchanging "word of God;" other texts are revised and expanded by later generations. Texts can be literal, or metaphorical, or both. One of the oldest known religious texts is the Kesh Temple Hymn of ancient Sumer, a set of inscribed clay tablets which scholars typically date around 2600 B.C.

The 2150 B.C. Epic of Gilgamesh from Sumer stands as the earliest text including various mythological figures and themes of interaction with the devineE (the dating notation, B.C. is the same as BCE-before common era)

The Rig Veda of Hinduism is estimated to have been composed between 1700-1100 B. C. and is the earliest text still used in religious practice today.

There are many possible dates given to the first writings which can be connected to Talmudic and Biblical traditions, the earliest which is found in scribal documentation of the 8th century B.C. Common traditional Judaic Christian earliest dating ranges from16th-12th century B.C. Others date the earliest from 900 B.C.-450 B.C.

High rates of mass production and distribution of religious texts did not begin until the invention of the printing press in 1440 A.D. before which all religious texts were hand written copies of which were relatively limited quantities in circulation.

Associated Terminology

A religious canon refers to a generally accepted, uniform, and often unchanging collections of texts which a religious denomination considers comprehensive in terms of their specific application of texts. For example, the content of a

Protestant Bible may differ from the content of a Catholic Bible. The word "canon" comes from the Sumerian word meaning "standard".

The terms "scripture" and variations such as "Holy Writ", "Holy Scripture" or "Sacred Scripture" are defined by the Oxford English Dictionary as terms which specifically apply to Biblical text and the Christian tradition. Hierographology or Hierology is the study of sacred texts.

Traditional Christian Canon

For Protestantism, this is the 66-book canon. Some denominations also include the 15 books of the Apocrypha between the Old Testament and the New Testament, for a total of 81 books. For Catholicism, this includes seven deuterocanonical books in the Old Testament for a total of 73 books, called the Canon of Trent (in versions of the Latin Vulgate, 3 Esdras and 4 Esdras are included in an appendix, but considered non-canonical).

For the Eastern Orthodox Church, this includes the anagignoskomena, which consist of the Catholic deuterocanon, plus the Maccabees, Psalm 151, the prayer of Manasseh, and 3 Esdras. 4 Maccabees is considered to be canonical by the Georgian Orthodox Church.

The Ethiopian Orthodox Tewaedo Church (and its offspring, the Eritrean Orthodox Church) adds various additional books.

Other Faiths

The Buddhist canon consists of the Sutras: the words and teaching of the Buddha. A number of non-canonical texts; referring to rules of conduct and states after death. Zen

Buddhists have no "sacred texts" in that "nature is transcending intellect."

The Sacred texts of Hinduism: The Vedas, or "Books of Knowledge," are the foremost sacred texts. Two texts: stuti (heard), and smruti (remembered), One divine-the other from the sages.

As the third of the Abrahamic religions, Muslims respect the Old and the New Testaments. Their two major sacred writings: The Quran and Hadith (the deeds of Mohammed and his followers). Muslims often refer to the three Abrahamic traditions as the "People of the Book".

Judaism:

The Jewish Bible; Tanakh, consisting of three sections, The Pentateuch, the Prophets and The Writings. Note: The Israel Ministry of Foreign affairs offers a comprehensive explanation of Judaism's sacred texts.

Religion and "Hell"

According to recent Pew poling about 80% of evangelical Protestants believe in hell, along with 76% of Muslims and 63% of Catholics. Even 27% of those who identify as 'nones'—the religiously unaffiliated—retain a belief in hell. And then there is the 1 percent who don't believe in God at all but still believe in hell.

Not every tradition features eternal damnation. The Hebrew Scriptures have scant hints about afterlife of any kind. So, it makes sense that Jews are split 80/20, with a majority rejecting the existence of hell. For the Hindus and Buddhists, hell is more a way station than a final destination.

C. S. Lewis felt compelled to soften the concept. Lewis'

literary depiction of hell is not a lake of fire but a grey suburb in which it is always raining, and nothing is satisfying and everyone quarrels with the neighbors. For Lewis, hell is eternally by those consumed by egotism. "The doors of hell", he said, "are locked from the inside."

Where Major Religions Stand on Same-Sex Marriage

Against:
Episcopal Church
Evangelical Lutheran Church in America
Presbyterian Church (U.S.A)
Reform Jewish Movement
Society of Friends (Quaker)
Unitarian Universalist Association of Churches
United Church of Christ
American Baptist Churches
Assemblies of God
Church of Jesus Christ of Latter-day Saints (Mormons)
Islam
Lutheran Church-Missouri Synod
National Baptist Convention
Orthodox Jewish Movement
Roman Catholic Church
Southern Baptist Convention
United Methodist Church
Christian Churches (Disciples of Christ)
Independent Christian Churches
Churches of Christ

Religion... can also be funny
*Memories of a retired pastor; (*Not this author*)*

"As a young minister, I was asked by a funeral director to

hold a grave-side service for a homeless man, one with no family or friends. The funeral was to be held at cemetery way back in the country, and this man was to be laid to rest there.

As I was not familiar with the backwoods area, I became lost and being a typical man did not stop for directions. I finally arrived an hour late. I saw the backhoe and the crew, who were eating lunch, but the hearse was nowhere in sight.

I apologized to the workers for my tardiness, and stepped to the side of the open grave, where I saw the vault lid already in place. I assured the workers that I would not hold them up for long, but this was a proper thing to do. The workers gathered around, still eating their lunch. I poured out my heart and soul.

As I preached the workers began to say "Amen," "Praise the Lord," and "Glory." I preached and I preached like I'd never done before; from Genesis all the way to Revelations. I closed the lengthy service with a prayer and walked to my car.

As I was opening the door and taking off my coat, I overheard one of the workers saying to another, "I ain't never seen anything like that before and I've been putting in septic tanks for twenty years."

Religion and Humor

One must understand that humor has always been part of a healthy appreciation of religion and its institutions. When theological, transcendent, and metaphysical discussions become too academic, many loose interest very quickly. However, humor can often probe the essence of religious concepts and entertain at the same time. Many religious writers and speakers employ humor as an "emotional warm up' making sometimes 'tough to hear' messages more palatable while allowing the listener or reader to 'let down his/her guard' allowing the message to more freely find a receptive audience. In another sense, illustrations can also create similar receptivity.

Pastor, Joel Osteen, leads one of the nation's largest churches in Houston, Texas. His Sunday sermons always begin with a brief joke. Along with his preaching without notes, his humor and simple life challenges messages have made him a favorite with both his 34,000 weekly attendees and a worldwide TV audience .. One of his recent jokes: "Two old friends died on the same day and went to heaven. These neighbors constantly argued about whether God was white or black. They were even quizzing St Peter about it when Jesus walked up with a welcoming, "buenos deos."

Following are some of my favorite religious 'jokes'. To identify each underlying religious concept would be somewhat demeaning to my savvy readers.

A fellow was late to a meeting with the parking lot full. He started praying, "Lord, if you can find me a parking slot, I'll start going to church again." Suddenly a car pulled out right in front of him. "Never mind lord, I found one."

A 1ˢᵗ grade teacher to her class: "If you can tell me what you did at recess and write it on the board, I'll give you a lollipop." Johnny Jones; " I played in the sand box." The teacher; "fine, write 'sand' on the board." He did and she handed him a lollipop. Mary Smith;" I played with Sue in the sand box." .. "fine, write 'box' on the board." Lollipop.

Billy Goldberg: "Well, I tried to play in the sandbox and Johnny and Mary threw rocks at me." "What!!, sounds like anti-Semitism. Shame on you two. Billy, if you can write anti-Semitism on the board you'll get a lollipop."

'Light bulb' Jokes.

How many Calvinists does it take to change a light bulb?

A: None, God has predestined when the light will go on.

How many Pentecostals does it take to change a light bulb?

A: 10, one to change and nine others to pray against the spirit of darkness.

How many Episcopalians.....................light bulb?

A: 10, one to change the bulb and 9 to say how much they liked to old bulb.

How many Presbyterians...............light bulb?

A: 1, Well, it should require about five committees to review the idea first. If each is staffed with half a dozen members, ... that's what, 30?

How many Church of Christ members...........light bulb?

A: 1, and four others to serve refreshments

How many Charismatics .... light bulb?

A: 3; one to change it and two to catch it when it falls.

How many fundamentalists .... light bulb?

A: The Bible doesn't say anything about light bulbs.

How many Quakers .... light bulb?

A; 10 to sit around in a circle until one feels the light.

How many Independent Baptists .... light bulb?

A: Only one; any more than that would be considered to be ecumenical.

How many Mormons .... light bulb?

A: One man and four wives to tell him how to do it.

How many Methodists .... light bulb?

A: Undetermined; whether your light is bright, dull or completely out, you are loved. You can be a light bulb, turnip bulb, or tulip bulb. Church wide lighting service is planned for Sunday. August 19. Bring bulb of your choice and a covered dish.

How many Lutherans .... light bulb?

A: None, Lutherans don't believe in change.

How many Amish ...... bulb?

A: What's a light bulb?

How many Independent Christian Church members bulb?

A: Hard to say. We don't have any official way of determining how to change a light bulb, but let's wait and see what Pastor Billy Bob has to say at the convention.

How many Disciples of Christ members .... bulb?

A: Let's first see what the Methodists have to say about it.

How many Catholics ...... bulb?

A: We don't use bulbs, we use candles.

How many Episcopalians .... bulb?

A: Not sure of the costs. Let's see if we can convince the two others on the city council to fund it. And besides, our people do not climb ladders.

How many Muslim apologist spokespersons .... bulb?

A: Two; one to make sure nobody blames Islam for it having burned out, and another to tell people they're being Islamophobes if they notice that it has gotten dark.

How many atheists .... bulb?

A: None, because can't the light bulb just change itself? What's that? It can't? Oh well look at that. I guess nothing happens without a cause huh? Stupid us

A Few More Religious Jokes

A drunk gets on a local bus. So shaky he couldn't seem to find his fare. Finally, very irritated, the driver floorboards the bus sending the man flying down the aisle with his ending up falling in a heap on a seat next to a solemn, somewhat disgusted man who was wearing a tall black hat and a clerical collar.

The drunk gazing up at the man, in very blurred speech, "Who are you?"
Responding the man sternly answered, "I am a Dunkard Pastor."
"Funny, that's what the bus driver called me."

A priest, rabbi and a minister walk into a bar.
The bartender looks up and says, "What is this, a joke?."

In rather a loud voice, a pastor was railing at the close of his Sunday morning message, "if I had all the beer in the world, I would throw it into the river. If I had all the whiskey in the world, I would throw it into the river."

As he was being seated, the music director got up and announced the closing hymn, "Shall we gather at the river."

And finally, a sign: COME WORK FOR TIIB LORD, THE WORK IS HARD, LONG HOURS, PAY IS LOW, BUT THE RETIREMENT BENEFITS ARE OUT OF THIS WORLD

Religious News Briefs

Persecution seems to be the number one religious news item. However, uplifting reports continue demonstrating faith's generosity, acceptance, openness and the reaching of hands of unity across mistrusting chasms, once so deep, very few even tried.

Recent Headlines;

Hindu vigilantes increase attacks on India's Muslims.
210

Opposition lawmakers cite 'climate of fear' A group called the Hindu Youth Brigade entered a house and pulled out a young Muslim man and a Hindu woman. Their offence: They were an interfaith couple in love. They beat the man, videotaped the incident and turned him over to police for charges of obscenity. Attacks similar to this are increasing in this overwhelmingly Hindu country after the gains made by the ruling Hindu Nationalist Bharatiya Janata Party (BJP) in early 2017. A leader for the Nationalist Congress said Muslims feel a deep sense of dread, since a Hindu nationalist took office 2014. Another leader is quoted saying, " They are seeking to impose a single uniform ethic ... whether it is in relation to food, dress, culture or thinking." A BJP spokesman: "This propaganda ... unreal, fabricated, fictional." World religions continue to make news in the 21" century. One might have added, "fake news".

Terrorism is grim reality for Coptic Christians.

U.S. church mourns 44 killed in Egypt attacks, the latest in a long history of suffering. The message was all too familiar to those attending morning services at the Coptic Orthodox Church of St Mark in Jersey City. The Islamic State claimed responsibility for two terrorist attacks on Coptic churches in the Egyptian town of Tanta. The bombing hit close to home in that many of the parishioners had loved ones and friend who died in the attacks. One of the clergy remarked that the morning prayer included, "We don't ask for vengeance. We pray that the blinds are taken off their eyes and they can see again." That is always the message. The Coptic Orthodox Church was founded by the Gospel writer Mark in the years after the death of Christ and broke free from the Roman Catholic Church

400 years later. The Copts have their largest base of support in Egypt and Northern Africa and many have established a presence in the United States.

Pope Francis is open to allowing married men into priesthood. Some remote areas are desperate for religious leaders. The pope raised the idea in an interview with the German newspaper, Die Zeit. He ruled out the prospect of allowing single men who are already priests to marry but was open to the idea of allowing unmarriied laymen or men already married to be ordained.

The Vatican accepts married priests in certain circumstances such as those in Eastern Rite sects of the church, and married members of the Anglican or Episcopal churches who convert to Catholicism.

WORLD Religion	Adherents	Percentage
Christianity	2.2 billion	31.50%
Islam	1.6 billion	22.32%
Secular Agnostic/Atheist	<1.1 billion	15.35%
Hinduism	1 billion	13.95
Chinese Traditional Religion	394 million	5.50%
Buddhism	376 million	5.25%
Ethnic Religions	300 million	4.19%
African Traditional Religions	100 million	1.40%
Sikhism	23 million	0.32%
Spiritism	15 million	0.21%
Judaism	14 million	0.20%
Baha'i	7.0 million	0.10%
Jainism	4.2 million	0.06%
Shinto	4.0 million	0.06%
Cao Dai	4.0 million	0.06%

Zoroastrianism	2.6 million	0.04%
Tenrikyo	2.0 million	0.02%
Neo-Paganism	1.0 million	0.01%
Unitarian Universalism	0.8 million	0.01%
Rastafarianism	0.6 million	0.01%
Total	**7,167 million**	**100%**

The Bible: Origin, Authority, Interpretation

Conflict about how to see and read the Bible is the single greatest issue dividing Christians in north America today. One side of the divide are fundamentalists and many conservative-evangelical Christians. On the other side are moderate-to-liberal Christians, mostly in mainline denominations. Positions on critical aspects of the division follow:

1. The origin of the Bible.
   Group one; the conservatives Group two; the liberals.
   Group one: believe that the 4th century Christian leaders who selected those books that were to be included in the canon were inspired by God to reject all heretical texts and

to accept the books whose authors were inspired by God, and whose texts were inerrant.

Group two: believe that the leaders that selected the books chose those that more closely matched their own beliefs. The three book, Matthew, Mark and Luke were chosen because they harmonized well with each other and with the beliefs of the fourth century church. The gospel of John had a more difficult time being accepted because some viewed it as having excessive Gnostic content. After finally being accepted, with reluctance, it profoundly changed the beliefs of the Christian movement thereafter.

2. The authority of the Bible:

Group one: believe God inspired the authors, and the text is inerrant.

Group two: Believe the Bible to be a human document, not inerrant. View it as an evolving belief system.

3. Interpretation; Group one: word of God; free from error, at least in the original version written by the authors. They accept that and allow that some copying errors and rare insertions of forged texts. Take what might be called a "top down" approach The Bible's purpose is for God to communicate religious and spiritual truths to humanity; cannot be understood by natural man; only after one is saved with God coming into his life making clear the meaning of the Bible

Group two: 'One of the world's important religious texts." Many of the parts cannot be taken literally, either as historically factual, or as expressing the will of God. Take a "bottom up" approach; the Bible being a human response to God. In an early ministry, this writer remembers a mainline Pastor advertising, "The Bible is our Roadmap." Yes, but hardly a rock of belief.

Chapter 14

A Positive Note

Lest a picture be painted too critical of old line religious institutions and their membership decline, there is a very positive note that such institutions strike; the wealth of historic charity giving.

A brief look at the major religions' charitable efforts reveals surprising generosity from both institutions and individual donors. Following are their primary charitable agencies:

Lutherans:
Charity; Lutheran Social Ministry.

Episcopalians;
Most of their charity work is done congregationally, often in concert with other organizations such as, Love Inc.

Methodists:
After medical indigent patient's medical bills exceed 10% of patient's annual income, Methodists Healthcare will in most cases pay the balance of the bill. The Methodists have eleven hospitals nationwide.

Jewish:
The Jewish Federation of North America. Inter Association of Jewish free loans.

Salvation Army Centers.
Y.M.C.A.

With charity centers in most states
Christian Churches (Disciple of Christ):

Disciple Mission Fund: supports 72 Ministries worldwide.

Reconciliation Ministry

Week of Compassion; One annual Sunday offering that supports their Charitable giving.

Independent Christian Churches and Churches of Christ:

Because these 15,000 U.S. congregations are independent there is no central charitable agency. Individuals, single congregations and Alliances contribute to and manage hundreds of such ministries.

Baptists:

Baptist World Charities;

Just one of many such organizations

BWC's Motto for world relief:

If I can go, I will go

If I cannot go, I will send.

But I refuse to sit and watch

Adventists:

Adventist Development and Relief Agency;

Ranked among the top 200 largest U.S. charities with 93.2% spent on program expenses.

Jehovah's Witnesses:

The Watch Tower Society uses 90% of all donations for disaster relief and the publishing of their Bibles and Bible aids.

Muslims:

Muslim Aid and Islamic Relief: British survey reports; Muslims (per capita) giving to both Islamic and non-Islamic charitable causes; 75% higher than Atheists' giving; 50% higher than both Catholic and Protestant giving; 30% higher than Jewish giving;

Evangelicals:

The Evangelical Council of Financial Accountability (ECFA) reports that in 2012 charitable giving to 1600 of its accredited organizations rose by 6.4% to 11 billion dollars over that recorded in 2011.

Government and Religion Charitable Alliances

The U.S. government along with other national governments have supported religious charitable institutions in critical ways. A good example of this cooperation through senior care centers. HUD program 232, is a government funding program providing financing for churches and other non-profit organizations that want to serve older seniors in one of four models of facilities; the most in demand; the Assisted Living facility. With 35 year fixed low interest rates (currently 4-4.5%), and up to 95% of loan to value these loans are very attractive. Any 'profits' may be used to support the sponsoring church's ministry. Typically, and currently, the minimum program (unless circumstances dictate otherwise): 60 rooms, $8M model. Current national average; room/suite for two, annual rental rate, $43,000.

Religion's Next Chapter

A Christian viewpoint .... there is no final chapter.

As a young Pastor, I was greatly influenced by the writings of J. Wallace Hamilton, Pastor of the Pasadena

Community Church in St. Petersburg, Florida. Being reared and educated in strong religious conservatism, his messages deeply challenged me to see a much larger world with needs both religious and social that I had either consciously chosen to ignore or subliminally relegated to the non-critical. Hamilton was, by some reports, representative of the growing Social Gospel movement. If so, he was ce1tainly a compelling and eloquent representative. He might be called a prophet fairly describing the abiding social ills of his day and projecting today's social upheavals while always applying "the good news."

This closing chapter builds upon both the primary religious and social challenges remaining through the decades of this century. We must answer the question of why religious division remains a crippling testimony to spiritual "oneness". Then we must search for a solution not only to this 'spirit of divisiveness' but also lifting that freedom and ultimate victory that God has offered to all.

When you have no god, you make one. Man has always done that. When he wanted to get drunk he made a Bacchus. When he wanted to fight he made Mars, Thor and others to give sanction to his vengeful spirit. The gods man makes always suits his convenience. They are created out of nothing to give supernatural sanction to his opinions and passions, or to support the political schemes he has devised for his own self-interest.

The Romans, for example needed something cohesive to hold together the scattered peoples of their empire, so they made a god of their emperor; "Worship Caesar!" The Japanese had no national faith to unite them, so they manufactured one. They dusted off an old nature religion, Shintoism, and linked it up with the emperor, "the son of heaven"—presto! **political monotheism**. It's a quick trick.

It's never pretty because nine out of ten times the gods we make are the deifications of our sins. Then one day the God who made us gets into the picture and there is a clash-and a decision must be made.

That is what Elijah was doing on Mt. Carmel-forcing a decision. "How long will you go limping with two different opinions? If the Lord is God, follow him. But If Baal, then follow him." Who was Baal? What was Baalism?

We're wrong to think that the controversy between God and Baal was only a feud between rival deities. Baalism was a system, an economic, political system; an ideology-a way of life. Reflect for a moment on the statement in the beginning of this book, *"Money is the basis for all physical events; it is the bartering of goods and services that move all material events."* An old Jewish doctor shared with me his philosophical take on life, "All 'worldly' enterprises, especially wars, are the result of economic forces. You have what I want and possessing greater financial strength, I will take yours."

This ideology grew out of an old attitude; the owner of land rules. The word baal means "OWNER" and in the beginning had nothing to do with religion. A slave's master was called a baal; a prince who controlled a fortified city or had large land holdings was called a baal; and let's not forget that a woman's husband was called her baal, her owner. Gradually the word became synonymous with the aristocracy, the upper class who owned the land, lived in the castle on the hill and had slaves to do the work for them. It came to be a religion when the land-owning aristocracy needed supernatural sanction to support their system and invented a god to fit it. They got the idea across that Baal was the god of fertility, good crops, and prosperity. Their 'theological' principle was that a few were ordained to own the land and exercised authority over the many, and that the many were ordained to work the land and be servants of the few. That was the accepted ideology of Baalism.

Into that situation came the Hebrews with a different opinion or theology. Not ownership but stewardship. In their faith, authority was vested not in princes but in God. He was the great king before whom high and low stood as subjects. He was the owner, the Baal, and the earth was the Lord's.

A land holding aristocracy was prohibited by the Laws of Moses. Man was a tenant, holding his land in trust and his lease expired every fifty years (the year of Jubilee). His taxes were paid, not to an earthly baal, but to God-one tenth, a tithe of his production, administered by the priests. No class distinction was allowed in Israel.

The Hebrew commonwealth was the germ-seed, the forerunner, of what is called "democracy." It was a way of life in which the rights of man were safeguarded.

The issue that gives point to Elijah's challenge: the Hebrews were always losing faith in their faith and forsaking their own disciplines to copy those of their pagan neighbors. It made Elijah angry. Then his challenge," how long ...... if you want to be heathen, go along with Baal."

Quoting from Hamilton: "History is a story of two points of view. One, that the earth belongs to a few at the top, while many are made to the servants of the few. On the other side is the way of God, rooted in the principle of stewardship; the earth is the Lord's and all men stand equal before Him; the eai1h is lent to men for a little while so that through brotherhood and mutual service they might build upon it the Kingdom of God."

From Moses and the exodus from Egyptian slavery, to that night in Bethlehem, to this people prepared through a thousand years with a concept of human freedom and dignity, came Jesus. He was not born in a castle but a stable. He announced Himself as the Deliverer of the enslaved and the bearer of good news to the poor. The common people heard him gladly. It was a divine blast to the whole castle-on-the-hill philosophy-small wonder it made a cross for Him.

The Roman Empire into which Jesus was born, was baalism lifted up to national proportions. Rome was the owner, the big baal sitting high on her seven hills with her foot on the neck of the world; a colossal world-aristocracy built upon the enslavement of the many for the enrichment of the few.

One must not forget that Christianity was a movement almost wholly among the lower classes of society. It was headed by a carpenter with a band of peasants, and its recruits were almost wholly from the lower strata of society. The history of the first four centuries is the growing uprising of the world's common people, people who came to believe in themselves because they believed in Christ. As the castle towers began to collapse, Constantine reluctantly made Christianity the state religion in response to the mightiest surge of the 'democratic' spirit since the days of Moses. The common man had found a great and hopeful faith.

Not too long after, the Middle Ages found a new Baalist in Feudalism, first in Europe and then to the Americas, followed by Africa and southeastern Asia. The big house on the hill was again its ideology. The church itself was swallowed up in its own Baalism.

It should be noted that there is a resurgence of the 'common man' church movement where no allegiance is giver to ecclesiastical oversight. While mainline heavily regulated denominations are losing members and sagging attendance is economically pressuring, the opposite is true among independent churches.

An old adage: the Episcopalians own the city; the Presbyterians run the city and the Baptists enjoy the city.

Lest we feel too smug about our 'democracy', let us ask ourselves some questions. What happened to the North American Indian and to those black men and women the slave ships brought to do the work no one else was willing to do? Present day examples are far too many.

The Great Compulsion

For many, quoting the 'Great Commission' is about as far as they go in the "go ye therefore " admonition. John's gospel tells us that ...**"he (Jesus) must go through Samaria."** Let your mind wrap around this picture. Jesus talking to a woman by a well side in Samaria, talking about eternal life. Here you have the whole world picture. Here is the problem and the answer. Here is the blueprint of the church's task. Here is the great compulsion that was in the heart of Christ and must be in the hearts of those who bear His name in this

To some who say this episode never happened, they insist she would have never engaged in this conversation. What made the difference? Jesus spoke as no teacher before him treating every person with dignity and always expected on something in everyone, even the lowliest, "...he must...go through Samaria."

This scene played out in a background of a bitter, age long religious feud. The Jews would have no dealings with the Samaritans. Josephus, the Jewish historian, described that background quite frankly. He said that when the northern Jew wanted to go to Jerusalem he always made a detour around Samaria which lay directly between Galilee on the north and Judea on the south. He was not interested in the shortest distance between two points. But not willing to lay all the blame on the Jews, he indicated that the Samaritans themselves provided the Jews some other reasons for making the detour. Jewish pilgrims had been waylaid on their way to their national festivals while passing through Samaria. For many years it was neither desirable nor advisable for a Jew to go through Samaria.

"...He must go through Samaria." He would not perpetuate a problem that had been created by man's sin, narrowness and resentment. On the journey Jesus had a conversation with a woman, something which dismayed his disciples. Tradition, custom and religion were against it. Besides, the woman was also a sinner. Jesus was always ahead; the living herald of the dawn.

Coming down a dusty road was a woman, not much of a woman, not a college professor, rather a hopeless woman with her head down and life tangled headed for Jacob's well. Jesus, there under a shade tree startled the woman with a question, "Suppose you give me a drink"? And then the conversation.

Though Samaritan women came daily to the well, tradition expected their heads to be held low; to speak to a strange man forbidden, there is something to be said about women's natural curiosity.

Respond to the very highest truth. Jesus believed in people, and they believed in him because He believed in them.

It is right to desire better standards of living for all people, but when we make that the end and goal of life we are only repeating the folly of the rich fool who tried to find his heaven in a bigger and better barn.

This woman had made a mess of her life having tried all its empty wells. Married five times, sounds like a modern

Hollywood story. Remember that which the Man at the well said, "Whosoever drinketh of this water shall thirst again; But whosoever shall drinketh of the water I shall give him shall never thirst; the water ... shall be in him; a well of water springing up into everlasting life."

The first thing he had to do was to deal with her sins. "Go call your husband," he said. Notice, He didn't say I'll give you a year's supply of water pots. Instead imagine Jesus leading her mind up out of the darkness into the light. It is no accident that Jesus is called "the Savior." Her new life began as she trusted Him and His words leading her to follow Him down a whole new path. "The woman left her water pot and went into the city and said .... "Come see a man..... is not this the Christ?" What began as a conversation over a water pot ended up in a spiritual awakening of a village.

A long procession of people walking the roads of Samaria, have looked into His face and can never be the same again; people coming out of yawning prisons with the New Testament in their hands; people coming across those Roman roads with a bit of good news on their lips; "Come, see a man!"; exiles and refugees marching across Europe with the seeds of the Reformation in their hearts; oak-hardened pioneers climbing up the slopes of the new England saying if they couldn't raise anything else there, they would raise men and women following the old wagon trails across America because "their eyes had seen the glory of the coming of the Lord."

Why do men live as if God were dead? **God's loving touch upon the spirit is not an old story; it still happens**. Something has been started that can never be stopped; forces have been released that can never be exhausted.

He has sounded forth the trumpet that shall never call retreat;
He is sifting out the hearts of men before His judgment-seat:

O, be swift, my soul, to answer Him! Be jubilant, my feet!
Our God is marching on.

How much we need an Elijah to shake us, to challenge us: "If this is the way of God, stay with it, stand for it. If the Lord be God, follow Him!" Today we are caught halfway between fear and hope. We know what's going, but we don't yet know what's coming. We can't help sighing over much of the past that was romantic, even in its wrongness. Neither can we return to it. The man or nation who would be master in the world must learn now to be the servant. The man in the castle must bow now to the Man born in a stable.

Here then is the compulsion: we too MUST go....

Recommended Resources

Rhodes, Ron; The Challenge of the Cults, Zondervan Colson, Charles; Kingdoms in Conflict, Zondervan Sacred Writings; The Harvard Classics, P. F. Collier Martin, Walter; The Kingdom of the Cults, Bethany Fellowship The Dictionary of Cultural Literacy, Houghton Mifflin (2nd addition)Catechism of the Catholic Church, 1997, Doubleday Tomlinson, L. G.; Churches of Today, Gospel Advocate Mead, Frank S.; Handbook of Denominations, Abington Press Ropp, Harry; The Mormon Papers, Inter Varsity Fellowship Lawson, Leroy; The New Testament Church, Then and Now,

Standard Publishing
Jenkins, Jerry and LaHaye, Tim; Left Behind, Tyndall house Elliott, David Vaughan; Nobody Left Behind Shannon, Robert; The New Testament Church, Standard Publishing Religion, Etymology and History Wikipedia; Primitive Religion; Mystery Cults, Collies Encyclopedia; History of Religion, Encyclopedia Britannica, University of Chicago Edwards, Jonathan; The Preacher, Baker Book House Canright, D. M.; Seventh-Day Adventism, Revell Company Islam Holy Books; Quran, (The Recitation), The Five Pillars. Urban, H. B.; A History of a New Religion (Scientology)

Princeton University Press
Calvin, John; The Institutes of the Christian Religion, Piper, John; Arminianism vs. Calvinism, Web article Barclay, William; The Daily Study Bible, The Westminster Press

Introduction to Revelation;
The Gnostic Heresy (Colossians) Holy Bible; New International Version, Zondervan
The New Testament from 26 Translations; Zondervan

96798569R00145

Made in the USA
Columbia, SC
02 June 2018